DATE DUE

			Printed in USA

HIGHSMITH #45230

Powell Lectures on Philosophy
at Indiana University
W. HARRY JELLEMA, EDITOR

———

SEVENTH SERIES

———

AMERICA'S PROGRESSIVE PHILOSOPHY

AMERICA'S PROGRESSIVE PHILOSOPHY

BY

WILMON HENRY SHELDON

SHELDON CLARK PROFESSOR OF PHILOSOPHY, YALE UNIVERSITY

Published for Indiana University

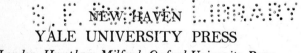

YALE UNIVERSITY PRESS
London, Humphrey Milford, Oxford University Press
1942

The Printing-Office of the Yale University Press

THE MAHLON POWELL FOUNDATION

MAHLON POWELL—1842–1928

WABASH, INDIANA

Extract from the last Will and Testament
of Mahlon Powell:

Having entertained a desire for many years to assist in the cause of a higher education for the young men and women of our state and nation, and to that end provide a fund to be held in trust for the same, and to select a proper school or university where the same would continue in perpetuity, I will, devise and bequeath all of the real and personal property that I possess and of which I die seized to the Trustees of Indiana University, Bloomington, Indiana, to be held by them and their successors in office forever, the *Income* only to be used and applied in the support and maintenance of a *Chair* in *Philosophy* in said institution, and to be dedicated and forever known as "The Mahlon Powell Professorship in Philosophy" of said University.

In accordance with the provisions of this bequest, the Trustees of Indiana University have established a Chair in Philosophy on The Mahlon Powell Foundation. Each year a Visiting Professor will be invited to fill this Chair. The seventh lecturer on The Mahlon Powell Foundation is Wilmon Henry Sheldon.

HERMAN B WELLS
President, Indiana University

CONTENTS

PREFACE

IF the following pages help in any degree to foster more of the search for livable truth and less for theoretical flaws in the enduring metaphysical systems, they are sufficiently justified. The writer cordially thanks the Department of Philosophy at Indiana University, and especially Professor Jellema and Dr. Stephens, for this opportunity to express convictions which he cannot but believe to be of fundamental importance for the cause of philosophy.

W. H. SHELDON

New Haven, Connecticut.

AMERICA'S PROGRESSIVE PHILOSOPHY

I

THE PERSISTING TYPES OF PHILOSOPHY

The Thesis Stated

FIRST of all, the meaning of our title: America's Progressive Philosophy. Are we praising ourselves too much? Does the title smack of provincialism?

As everyone knows, there has come to expression in recent years—say roughly in the last half-century and increasingly in that period—a general philosophy of life and of nature which emphasizes the role of change or process as fundamental to reality. We think of Bergson, S. Alexander, James, Dewey, Mead, Whitehead, and the like. Now, whether right or wrong, this philosophy is a big one. Whitehead has an elaborate metaphysic, epistemology and logic, besides an aesthetic and an educational theory. As for Dewey, he has written much on every branch of philosophy from logic to art and religion—and all know the influence of his theory of education. Both follow Hegel's

great example in extending their central idea
to the many aspects of the world and of human nature. And if these two men are by
common consent outstanding defenders of
process as an all-round philosophy, we note
that they matured it in the U.S.A. Even the
English Alexander, teaching emergent evolution in his admirable work, *Space, Time,
and Deity*, did not give to process the universality they have given it. Nor did Bergson, since he did not find real duration
characteristic of the inorganic realm. And
who does not see that the notion of process
naturally flourishes in our mental climate?
Yes, the process-philosophy, as we shall call
it, rounded and matured in this country
alone, and so persuasive, too, to many of our
younger thinkers, may fairly be dubbed our
distinctive contribution to the history of
thought.

But the title says *progressive* philosophy
too. And this cannot yet be justified: it is a
characteristic which will appear when we
study the system itself.

So much for the title. Now for the claim
we shall make. It is this: the process-philosophy is not only genuinely novel but also

fertile in a sense not yet realized. As novel, it furnishes an insight into the nature of reality which for depth and significance ranks it quite as high as the rival systems of idealism, scholasticism, materialism, etc.; an insight not given, at least explicitly, to these older views, and hardly to be expected until certain results of modern empirical sciences were at hand. But if its novelty gives it a respectable status among the influential systems, its fertility gives it, in a quite unique way, a superior status. Superior—note this—in a quite unique way. For, we shall urge, its superiority does *not* lie in its being able to refute its rivals. Rather it lies in being able to grant them all an equal truth, and a truth as good as its own. It does not, or need not, find its own novel insight any *truer* than those of the other systems. But that insight, we shall try to show—that new note of process—is more fertile just because it shows how the rival views may all be compatible with one another and with itself. For it reveals a certain principle of growth at the heart of nature; and growth means increasing compatibility of different functions. A man may combine interests which to a boy are mutually exclusive—play and work, prudence and courage, self-interest and service. All are intrinsically combinable; and so, by the lesson we draw from the principle of growth, are the truths of the several philosophies. And if the new note of process lays bare this possibility of reconciling old enemies, surely it is more fertile than any one of those older insights. For it thereby at least releases energy now consumed in unproductive refutation, energy which may be used to discover new perspectives and new truths not yet dreamed of in our systems. Thus, we shall maintain, process-philosophy has a welcoming and generous attitude, calling for cooperation to replace competition, and for new and venturesome points of view of the inexhaustible wealth of reality about us.

Well, this thesis of ours is a fine and high-sounding project, is it not? But now let us begin to temper aspiration with realism.

As a fact, the new philosophy is something of a welter. It isn't as clear-cut as the monist idealism or the personal idealism of today, still less so than modern neo-Thomistic scholasticism. If we have called it mature and big, no doubt it is in its early maturity and may

expect some modification. Precise definition
is hardly in order yet. What we shall do—
all that we can do—is to select certain empha-
ses it makes, generally regarded by its devotees as central, and take these as its essence. It is for the experts to judge whether
or not we have treated it fairly. Perhaps we
should put our claim thus: there are certain
ideas, traceable in the writings of eminent
defenders, which seem both novel and fertile
in the sense just described. For our present
interest is not in contemporary history, except as a means of suggesting ideas, but
rather in truth and significance.

In one respect indeed our project is mis-
representing the new view. We are going to
see in it the means of reconciling rival systems; yes, of reconciling this present one
with the others. But unfortunately that irenic
motive is far from being shared by all its
disciples. Again and again they write refutations of materialism, of idealism, and probably most of all of scholasticism. They point
to those views as hindrances to truth, as
fundamentally erroneous. Here we only say
that these earnest devotees are not using
their own principle as they could use it. They

are still too much under the sway of the old spirit of exclusion, of the incompatibility of one insight with its polar opposite. They have not quite begun to realize that their new insight is so rich that they can afford to be generous to opponents.

The Types of Philosophy

Obviously we cannot judge the new message fairly unless we set it out in contrast to other views. And all the more so in virtue of our purpose to show it as reconciler and reformer. For we shall certainly find the systems needing reconciliation.

But if we look over the history of philosophy, the number of systems is indefinitely great. We cannot deal with such a mass of material. It would perhaps not be so bad if we could only group all together into one, to set it over against our present one. But the systems themselves seem to forbid this. They all, to a greater or less degree, insist on refuting one another. And this is true today as in the past. Present-day systems are largely occupied in mutual refutation, just as of old. Such is the sorry spectacle that confronts the innocent seeker after truth who wants to learn from the past and present thought of expert thinkers. Small wonder that those whose philosophical instinct does not happen to be an all-consuming flame are quite discouraged and give up the metaphysical search. And if this were all, the search would be foredoomed.

But there is more. There is not just a hodge-podge of systems. The systems align themselves. They congregate into separate camps. The camps are not always clearly or precisely distinct, but still distinguishable and groupable about certain central ideas or nodes. We find idealist systems of various sorts, from Hindu Vedantist to Plato, Hegel, Leibniz, and the modern idealism flourishing today as strongly as ever these did. For the latter does flourish: witness the impressive work of Blanshard, Urban, Brightman, Ewing, and others. We find materialist systems from Hindu Çarvaka to Democritus, Hobbes, and present-day materialists such as Montague in his masterly work, *The Ways of Things*. We find the synthetic scholastic group starting from Aristotle, broadened and codified by Aquinas, more vigorous today than ever as neo-scholasticism. And so on. Let us repeat: there are perhaps no exact limits within which we can confine these schools. Samkya, Plato, Eriugena, Hegel, differ much. Democritus with his atoms, Hobbes with his "ratio is but oratio," Montague with mind as potential physical energy—how far apart these seem. And even today there are disagreements within each camp. Yet each group, however vague at the edge, is well enough defined at the center. Each swings about a certain pivot. The idealist vows that mind, the immaterial, is the one ultimate real; the materialist swears by the ultimate reality of physical things or events. So too the scholastic cherishes the fixed hierarchic order and scale of being with God as perfect source to which the scale of creatures approximates. And so on. So the systems arrange themselves in a few types, each hinged and centered about a certain node-view, as we might call it. Perhaps no system ever to be set forth will be a perfect case of its type—just as no man may ever live who is quite all that man should be, and no square or circle found in nature will ever be a perfect square or circle. But always we find approximations to these, and always we

find in history, as we still do today, systems
that are predominantly idealist in tone, predominantly materialist in tone, and so on.
Nor is this classification merely modern or
in any way provincial, as belonging to this
age or that. The classification is as old as the
systems; it turns on the issues about which
they fought most bitterly.

The situation is analogous to a man's shots
at a target. They center around the bull's
eye, though none may precisely hit it. And
in the long history of philosophy we find a
small number of fairly well-marked bull's
eyes.

What are they then? First, just names.
They are idealism, monistic or pluralistic,
materialism, rationalism, irrationalism, scholasticism, and finally the modern process-
view. These are well-accredited terms, whose
age-long associations—except for the last—
at once arise in the mind. When we philosophers hear them, our minds make specific
response: at idealism we begin to glow and
warm up, or on the contrary to bristle; the
like at materialism, and so on. We feel like
defending or attacking and we are prepared
to define them. They have more pungency

than precision, doubtless; but they are, and have long been, felt as deeply significant, significant of truth for the defender, of falsity for the other camps.

What then do these names mean? Here, as we were saying above, precision beyond a certain degree is impossible. But it is not needed. All we require is a rough workable statement bringing out the important positive claim of each type and its dissent from its rivals. If I want to break a stick with a hammer, I need not know *precisely* where to grasp the hammer: somewhere near the end is sufficient. So to understand these type-views; enough to hit the important, meaningful ideas, to see their bearings and consequences so far as they too are important, etc.

Idealism stands for the ultimate reality of mind or spirit, as distinguished from matter or body. It means by mind, above all else, something that possesses value and permanence. Mind is not the sort of thing that is here today and gone tomorrow, just ephemeral feeling, always subject to accidents that destroy it. Bodily things are unstable—the tree is blown down, the rock is smashed, the winds rage and cease. Mind has something of the eternal, ageless, spaceless about it. This is true alike of early Hindu forms, of Platonism, of modern Hegelian (monistic) and Leibnizian (pluralistic) forms. The Platonic Ideas, Brahm, the Absolute Spirit of Hegel, the conscious person-minds of personalism—these are values and immortal, above the gnawing tooth of time and circumstance. The theme is familiar and throughout history repeated in ever varying shapes.

It is a very old type, perhaps the oldest of all. It originated, probably, in the comments of Hindu thinkers upon the sacred texts, the Vedas, and so on. Thus it drew its animus from religion; it is at heart a religious attitude. It revolts from the miseries of life and seeks eternal peace and rest from the pains, uncertainties, and struggles of bodily existence. Its motive is a practical one; it seeks some stable good. No matter how theoretical and abstruse the arguments that later were used to prove the reality of Brahm and the unreality of spatial-temporal things, they took their origin from the search for a lasting peace, a security that could not be obscured by the veil of Maya. It was a matter of finding the right kind of life to live. True, it did not, as a rule, lead to the kind of living that we moderns call practical. It did not counsel men to build better houses, to conduct their business, to devise new means of transportation, discover healing drugs, or in any way improve the physical conditions of this life. Rather it found the good it craved in withdrawing from such tasks. But whether or not we may think this way mistaken, we must not forget that for this early idealism it was a matter of getting a certain direct experience, of sensing the unity of all things in Brahm, rather than a theoretical demonstration. They chose a definite line of conduct and felt as a result of it their own immediate union with the eternal one and good. At one extreme, this conduct was the bodily discipline of the Yoga; at the other the passive contemplation of the Atman; in both alike it was an experiment carried out in search of the indestructible value. That is why Radhakrishnan can say that India is a land of saints.

We need to dwell on this practical motive of early idealism, because it has become obscured by the western use of the term practical, and consequently many of us fail to see the perennial drive in human nature that

leads to this type of thought. It is the religious motive. Idealism would show us the
eternal good underlying the apparent misery,
injustice, and weakness incident to man's
lot. It would make us so sure of the presence
of this good that we could not be bowled
over by any catastrophe. True, later idealism
sought, on the whole, to make us sure by
logical rather than experimental demonstration. But the motive remains.

This change toward theoretical proof was
probably due to the Greek. The Greek attitude, in the high days of philosophy, was on
the whole not experimental but contemplative. For the train of thinkers from Thales
through Aristotle the criterion of truth was
not practical but theoretical. They were good
observers—Aristotle was a great empiricist
—and they argued by logical implication
from what they saw to what they believed
the eternal verities. They did not feel the
need of testing those verities in experience
to see if they showed their power over the
lives of men. True, the masters Plato and
Aristotle were deeply concerned to better
the human lot. They wrote long treatises on
politics, the ideal State, justice, and the other

moral virtues. But their typical method was *first* to demonstrate with absolute logical certainty what the ideal conduct is and *then* proceed to act on it. As our modern proverb says: Be sure you're right, then go ahead. They felt that reasoning, based no doubt on good observation of human nature, could of itself guarantee the truth. And so we find that Platonic idealism is not, like much of the Indian doctrine, *directly* a way of life. It is not verified, in the sense of tested by its efficacy in man's living. Rather we know beforehand that it *will be* efficacious and do not need to test it. By all means let man, if he would better his life, live in the light of the Ideas. Let him follow the ideals of wisdom, courage, temperance, justice. But those ideals are, in any case, eternal in the heavens. As Socrates says at the end of the *Republic*, the ideal State is laid up in heaven, even though it may never come on earth.

And yet this contrast of method between Greek and Oriental serves to emphasize the point just made: idealism is a search for supreme value, value not to be found in the shifting world of physical forms and events, but only in the immaterial realm, where mind and reason are at home. For Plato, the Idea of the Good is the head of the list of Ideas. His motive, the motive of all idealists, was to make men certain of the being of this highest good, and to point them to the means of securing it.

Now the contemplative attitude of the Greek mind dominated the succeeding European philosophy and still dominates it. When idealism, always latent in the medieval thought, comes out again into the open in the modern period in Germany, it is wholly a matter of logical implication in the observed facts of nature. No practical test of idealism's truth is required. Even the voluntarist Schopenhauer declares that he does not write to make men better but solely in the interests of a true account. The Hegelian way of truth is, as Hegel declared, the making explicit of the implicit; and the implicit is what is *logically* implied. As all know, the keystone of this idealism is that every element, every aspect of the world, really implies in its full meaning every other. To know the flower in the crannied wall, really to understand it, is to know what God and man is. Nothing is intelligible by itself alone.

To understand anything is to see it as part of a logical system. The practically good has turned into the logically sound and stable; that which cannot be denied because it is implied in each particular thing or event and equally implies each. This notion of the organic unity of all things, i.e., the absolute spirit or mind, as a rational implication, is the essence of this monistic idealism. Mind it is, because as supremely one system it overcomes the separation so characteristic of bodies in space and events in time. Idealism has become rationalism.

It would be a great mistake, however, to call it a pure a priori rationalism. A priori method it certainly uses, but not excluding empiricism. Hegel's initial category was being. He started with the real world. He took its being for granted just as any empirical scientist would. He made no attempt to prove a priori that there is such a world. Nor did he try to prove by epistemological analysis that doubt and error imply knowledge. He deliberately discarded Kant's attempt (or what he thought was Kant's attempt) to criticize the faculty of knowledge as a preliminary to its exercise. He compared such an attempt to "the error of refusing to enter the water until you have learnt to swim."[1] There is, properly speaking, no epistemology in Hegel. His system is just an extremely thoroughgoing investigation of the *meaning* of reality, of what is implied if reality is to be intelligible. True, he assumed that reality must be intelligible; he never thought that the claim of the irrationalists, the mystics, the sceptics, deserved serious consideration. The postulate or axiom of intelligibility he never doubted. But he took reality for granted all through. And notice, too, that he always brought the deduced categories down to the plane of the real world. He verified, or at least meant to verify, the *fact* of becoming, of measurable quantity, of substances, causes, purposes, and so on, *in* the world. He verified, or tried to verify, the logical necessity of the dialectic in the actual events of human political history, in the actual forms of human art, in the actual development of human religious institutions. His incredibly vast labors, in the posthumous works on the Philosophy of His-

1. William Wallace, translator, *The Logic of Hegel* (2d ed. Oxford, Clarendon Press, 1892), II, 84.

tory, of Fine Art, on the History of Philosophy, the Philosophy of Religion, etc., bear
witness to this empirical motive in his rationalism. We may think that his evidence was
not wholly sound. We may think that sometimes he forced the facts of history, of physics,
mechanics, biology, and so on, into his preconceived mold. But at least his heart was in
the right place. He *meant* to verify the truth
of the dialectic by the actual course of events
in the real world. And no doubt an impartial
survey of his findings will see a great deal of
truth in the dialectic. Even James, with all
his antipathy to Hegel, admitted that the
dialectic was fairly true as an empirical law.

It is needful to emphasize this empirical
motive in monistic idealism if we are to
judge it fairly. Many, perhaps most of its
critics today tend to interpret it as a quite
a priori scheme, pure intellectualism as
James called it. Such an extreme view leads
to an out-and-out rejection of the system as
a whole, and we fail to glean from it what
truth we might. Indeed, this sort of thing is
all too common among philosophers. They
are wont to take some other man's system,
find certain flaws in it, and then throw it

away bodily. The trouble is they are really looking for errors rather than truth. Errors we surely can find in all systems; but we can also find truth in most if not all, and it would be more profitable to our search to garner the positive results they have brought to light and fund them into a common capital, on which we may draw interest to finance further research.

Such then is the picture of Hegelian or monistic idealism. It survives today as a well-marked school or type. As mentioned above, it has eminent defenders. If they do not concern themselves so much with the deduction and verification of the whole categorial scheme, as did Hegel (and also the English Bosanquet), they argue fervently and strongly for reality as one systematic whole of necessarily connected parts, a whole whose thoroughgoing rationality and individuality give it the title of One Mind or Spirit. Probably the best recent statements of this type are Blanshard's two volumes, *The Nature of Thought*, and Urban's *Language and Reality* and *The Intelligible World*.

Idealism, we said, is above all animated by the search for the highest value. Following the Greek–European conviction that the contemplative way rather than the experimental is the proper way of demonstration, it uses the method of logical implication; by this means it rounds to the One Absolute Spirit, present in us all and through us all, in nature and in the mind of man. To realize the presence of this spirit in every detail of life, no matter how horrible or disgusting by itself, is then man's highest good. And after all, this thought comes back to the thought of the earliest Hindu school, the doctrine of Brahm. True enough, it has traveled by a different path. True enough, it uses many facts not known to the unscientific early Indian: the content of its argument is far richer. The idea of organism or system— what Hegel called the Notion—was probably quite unknown to the first idealists. And doubtless, for that reason, their account of Atman, the one reality identical in all things, would be called by our modern idealists more negative, less rich in meaningful content. Nevertheless both arrive at substantially the same final value: absolute spirit, immutable in infinite varying manifestations, peace supreme permeating all the lesser

goods and apparent evils. At their centers
the two views are one. The wheel has come
full circle. The keynote of Indian idealism,
earliest of philosophies perhaps, is sounded
again as strongly as ever. And we must add
that this is true in India too, where idealism
flourishes vigorously today. It is a perennial
type of thought, surviving the batterings of
centuries of refutation.

Note this carefully: we shall use it later.
Idealism of the monist sort is a type that has
survived through the long ages of man's
thought, and is as strong as ever today.

But there is another form of idealism,
which also dates back to early India and also
survives today. This is usually called pluralistic idealism or personalism. Historically it
seems to come a little later than the monist
form; and naturally, for it is, logically speaking, a revolt, though a mild one, against the
latter. Let us see how.

Idealism is a search for supreme value.
The search ends, let us suppose, with the
one absolute spirit. But we soon see that
there is an apparent loss here: it is not all
gain. As the drop of water loses its identity
in the ocean, so do you and I lose our person-

ality in the absolute One. And the individual person has a value in himself. So felt the pluralists of early India; so feel the pluralists of today. The one absolute may be the highest good, but not *all* goods. The Hegelian might answer that the individual person lives and moves and has his being only through the One; for the One is the organic unity of the many individuals. This will not satisfy the pluralist. He feels a value in each individual for himself, an *independent* worth, however small, in each person. It is the note of independence that he stresses. So he raises the issue between the opposites—monism and pluralism. He stands for something the monist is unwilling to grant: independence, ultimate plurality. Plurality the monist can accept, but not *ultimate* plurality. In this way certain idealists revolt from their original camp and set up an opposing one.

The point might be put in another way: perhaps more impressively. What sort of experience feels the all-pervading unity of Brahm, or the all-inclusive oneness of the Absolute? For the older view, whatever the experience be, it is not open to description.

Neti, neti, says the Indian. Inscrutable, says the modern. No, we cannot even call it a *conscious* experience: consciousness implies discrimination, comparison, an object and a subject. But no distinctions enter here. The mind or spirit, Brahm, the Absolute—these are spirit because they are value itself, but they are not conscious. They are altogether above the level of consciousness. And here the pluralist must revolt. What good, he asks, in an experience not actually felt? The pith and juice are gone. It is not an actually present good. It is not verified. It lacks the specific quality of the here and now. Such a value is no value apart from conscious experience. Not only the values of personality are lost in the One; *all* value is lost. And surely it is not hard to sympathize with this claim. It is the one–many issue again: the issue between the *ultimate* one and the *ultimate* many; the one ineffable superconscious and the many conscious minds.

So idealism from the very fact that is at bottom a religious philosophy, a search for the ultimate value, inevitably falls into two forms, between which the strife seems just as final and insoluble as between any other types. For certainly the claims seem incompatible.

It has been necessary to dwell so long on idealism because here the issues have become so confused in modern times. Owing to the prominence of epistemology, idealism has been interpreted in an epistemological sense, and the real message of it for metaphysics has often been missed. Epistemological idealism, so-called, is really quite irrelevant to metaphysical idealism. It argues that the known object is a state of the knower: the external world is my idea, or sense-datum, etc. Then the idealist is supposed to go on and draw from this the fact that the world is mind, as with Vedantist or Hegel. It seems like a very short cut to a tremendously significant conclusion—the justification of the aspiration of the ages after ultimate spirit, by just a little bit of epistemological analysis. But just as little a bit of reflection shows that this subjective or epistemological idealism has no bearing whatever. What if all the world is my idea, or yours, or all of ours together? Does mentality *of that sort* imply mentality in the sense of a one highest *value*, an eternal good shining through all vicissitudes of life and nature? Not in the least. No conclusion about the *nature* of our ideas, the *kind* of ideas they are, whether or not they involve one another in an absolute system or reveal ultimately distinct persons, can possibly be drawn from their being ideas. It may well be that those ideas all follow and bunch themselves, according to the laws of gravitation, electrodynamics, etc. Then they might as well be called the physical world. The idealist has gained nothing worth gaining by this seeming short cut. Nor if he were decisively refuted, and the realist proved correct, would he have lost anything. Suppose there is a real external world, independent of me as a knower or experiencer. I still have no assurance whether or not it is a world of persons, of blind physical forces, of high spiritual principle, of ultimate evil or good. No, the problem of knowledge has no relevance to idealism. We learn what reality is only by investigating reality. There is no short cut to metaphysics.

Come now to the second type of philosophy, materialism. Materialism may be called

the polar opposite of idealism. To common
sense, everything in the world is either mental or bodily; neither is the same as the other.
Your thoughts and feelings are *not* your
physical organism; the stones and sand are
not conscious thinkers. Minds find life and
health good, disease and death bad. But the
physical world knows no good or bad; it just
is. The contrast is between values and facts.
No matter how high your ideals, the world
of facts, the rain and sunshine, the trees and
animals, are here and now, and you have to
submit to their ways. You can't wish them
away when they are bad. There is at least
another sort of world than the ultimate real
envisaged by the idealist. And he has to admit it too, for he has to fight hard, he has to
train himself by Yoga or by long and difficult
contemplation, to reach the true view. The
world of Maya has power, great power.
Calling it illusion does not deny its actual
presence; the illusion is here, even if it is
not the truth. And the materialist is the man
who revolts against the one-sided view that
looks at the ideal good alone. And revolting,
he like most human beings, especially when
young, goes to the other extreme. In the

dualism of right versus might, he follows the call of might. The directness and the power of things as they are overwhelm his conviction, and he declares that the physical world is the ultimate reality.

Materialism is essentially a protest-view; a protest against idealism. Probably it originated after idealism, as a reaction against idealism's extreme claims. It is not quite in accord with the philosopher's first instinct; it is too near the level of common sense. The philosopher wants to go deeper than common sense. And so, even if materialism may turn out to be the truth, the philosopher will as a rule not favor it. It deals too much with the obvious; he wants the ultimate which in this suffering world is not at all obvious. That is why in the long history of philosophy there is more idealism than materialism. That is why idealism can give itself the laudatory title of the "Great Tradition." It is the orthodox view; to it materialism is the radical, the prodigal, the hard-boiled and hardheaded rebel. And no doubt, if idealism had not already seized the throne, thinkers would not have been stirred to that organized rebellion which is materialism. Thus

the warfare between these two types perpet-
uates itself.

To be sure, we who look at these hostile
camps from the outside can see justice, and
injustice too, in each position. Whichever
may be the truth, we must sympathize with
the lofty and courageous aim of the idealist.
So we all go back to study Plato, no matter
how often he is refuted. He warms our
hearts. On the other hand we feel that the
Platonist tendency to undervaluate the ap-
pearances is unfair to the countermotive of
plain fact, and we sympathize with the materialist in his protest. Also we of today like
to favor the underdog, and materialism has
been the underdog in philosophy. At the
same time the materialist is not without a
certain spiritual pride—shall we call it?—
when he dubs himself tough-minded and
hardheaded; a pride too which some idealists share, in reverse, as self-consciously
orthodox.

Do you ask, why mention these emotions?
They have nothing to do with truth. On the
contrary they have much to do with it. Where
one looks and what he looks for so largely
determines what he finds. If Columbus had

not looked westward, he would not have
found America. The stay-at-homes would
never have done it. If there were no idealists, we should have *no* conception of the
highest good. If there were no materialists,
we should not have discovered the activities
of glands, blood pressure, nerve conduction,
and the various other facts of organic response that accompany conscious phenomena.
Yes, the wish to prove a preconceived thesis,
even a dogma, is a fruitful source of discovery. All honor to these rival schools for
their emotional attitudes to truth.

But the trouble comes when each arro-
gates to itself the *ultimate* truth. Neither denies, of course, the apparent or proximate
reality of mind or body. The idealist admits
the physical world to be real, but only as a
certain limited or abstract aspect of the absolute spirit. He says then that he includes
what truth there is in materialism. So, too,
the materialist admits that there *are* conscious events and states, and that they are
very different from the simpler events and
states of inorganic things. But he says that
in the final analysis all conscious processes,
all thought and experience, all values, even

the highest, are functions describable wholly in physical terms. Thus each side, apparently very tolerant and synthetic, really claims for itself alone the *ultimate* truth. No amount of concession can meet so deep an opposition as this.

Let there be no mistake here. It sometimes sounds as if modern materialism were almost turning into idealism or at least dualism; as if its conception of physical being made the physical so almost immaterial that it is well-nigh mental. No such thing! The physical is always the physical and mind is only a special case of the physical. You may define matter in this or that way, and your definition may change with the changes in scientific knowledge; but matter remains matter and the laws of matter remain the laws of matter, even though their statement changes and their necessity turns into a statistical probability. Look at the history of materialism and see how the meaning of matter has altered. For a typical early materialist, Democritus, matter was the collection of hard chunks, atoms, indivisible and eternal. Thought too was of such atoms composed: but they were smoother and

moved more easily. *Solid stuff* was the notion. As time went on, the researches of
scientists gradually changed the definition.
Primary matter seemed to evaporate into a
stuffless force, an inertial mass, and finally
into energy, as today many would define it.
Is this definition of matter as energy a whit
less materialistic than the old notion of the
solid chunk? Clearly not. There is no suggestion of consciousness in the physicist's
formula $\frac{1}{2}mv^2$ or *mas*. The opposition is not
diminished.

Note finally that materialism, like idealism, has persisted through the ages and is,
so far as one can judge, quite as strong today
as ever. It is a perennial type. *The Ways of
Things* by Montague has presented its case
in a form brilliant, clear, and stimulating to
the student and at the same time keenly conscious of the difficulties confronting the materialist definition of consciousness. In this
work we find materialism far more strongly
argued than in any preceding book of the
present type. Montague's thesis of potential
energy is surely a new and fertile notion,
which at least brings consciousness and body
nearer together. Nevertheless this material-

ist would never admit the *ultimate* reality of mind in the idealist sense.

The opposition of the two types idealism and materialism is patent enough. Now what more natural than to frame a philosophy which does justice to each, so far as each points out some positive reality, while avoiding the extreme claim of each to *sole* possession of the real? Such a synthetic system ought to settle the quarrel, so long a grievous scandal, and by its adjustment of each element, body and mind, to a definite place in the total scheme, provide a new insight into the structure of reality. An enterprise of this nature, greater in its conception and detailed working out than anything hitherto attempted, was undertaken by the last of the Greek geniuses, Aristotle, and carried to full fruition, if the term is permissible of human thought, by St. Thomas Aquinas. It survives today, more vigorous even than in the palmy days of the thirteenth century, and its strength is shown in its adaptability to the novel discoveries of chemistry and biology. The system of Aquinas, with some slight modifications, may fairly be named the orthodox form of modern scholasticism—

neo-scholasticism. Minor differences of view
there are today, but there is enough agreement to constitute a larger core than we can
find in either idealism or materialism. Idealism at the fullest has an elaborate doctrine of
the categories: but present-day idealists are
more concerned with the central thesis of
spirit's ultimate reality than with codifying
a fixed doctrine of categories. The followers
of Hegel have not as a rule inherited his interests in the order of nature and history.
And materialism, being mainly a philosophy
of protest, has done little but argue for the
reduction of consciousness to some function
of the physical organism. It has no standard
system of the make-up of nature; no official
map of its material universe. The neo-Thom-
ist system, on the other hand—scholasticism
we call it—is a system of enormous spread,
due to its really synthetic character. For it *is*
a synthesis, as idealism and materialism are
not. These two do not give genuine or ultimate reality to both mind and body: scholasticism does so. The physical universe is
for it just as real, just as little illusory or
"appearance" as the mental and spiritual.
True, the physical has not as full a *degree* of

reality as the other, but it is as truly real. The corporeal forms in primary matter which make up stones, rivers, planets, trees, oceans, or stars are as real as the angels, though the wealth of content within them is far less. And their being is not dependent on the being of the mental and rational creatures that make up the higher grades, as in the idealist scheme. They all have a being of their own: once created by divine fiat—not by any logical implication compelling God to manifest Himself—there they are, real by themselves. True, there is an admirable order in nature, but it is an order due to God's power, not to any organic necessity in the bodies and minds and their laws. The dualism of the view makes it a real synthesis.

But more: it gives the system an enormous spread. Being a positive philosophy and no mere protest, it will not be content to re-assert the mind–body dualism of common sense. As a metaphysic, it will look for a principle or principles shared by both, something fundamental to all being; and if it finds such a principle, it will trace that principle acting throughout the world of matter and of mind. What is the natural clue to its discovery? Well, if the universe as a whole is divided into these two realms, isn't the mind–body relation most deeply character-istic of reality? And may we not expect to trace this same relationship throughout the length and breadth of things? Probably it will assume special forms within special regions: it will not look quite the same in material things as in minds. But it will be verifiable as the same fundamentally: and it will appear intrinsic to all being. What then is this relationship?

Take a simple case. I intend to whittle a block of wood into the shape of a toy boat, and the intention is present before I start whittling. The process of whittling and the finished boat, means and end, are all here in my mind now; they are the stimulus which starts me whittling and the energy that car-ries me on till the boat is done. They are the active agencies of the situation. But the boat will never be made until my hands do the cutting. They are capable of it, they know how to wield a knife and to carve the wood into shape. They are potential whittlers. And my desire and choice to whittle are the act which makes them more than potential, makes them actual whittlers and makes the boat actual. Now here the mind is the active force—*act* as it is technically named—and the body (the hand) contains the *potency* which my mind turns into a real event. Now this sort of thing—our intentional action—is typical of conscious human life. Minds and their purposes are the active agents that bring out the potential capacities of our bodies. Mind is to body as act is to potency. Here is the clue we were looking for.

Now the scholastic traces this pair, act-potency, throughout the universe so far as known to man. He verifies its presence by evidence drawn from common observation and the sciences. Of course, it has a different look in the inorganic from that of life and mind. In nonliving things it appears as just substantial form and primary matter. The *substantial form* of lead or iron is the seat of the chemical forces (we should say electro-dynamic forces, but there is no difference of principle) which are shown in the reactions of these elements to other elements and their physical properties generally. The *matter* of lead and iron is the stuff (call it mass or energy if you prefer) which embodies these

forces; *they* are the active agents, *it* is simply
the passive recipient capable of receiving and
displaying them here and now, there and
then. As just matter it is thus pure potentiality. Since pure potentiality without some
actual behavior is just nonexistence, primary
matter is never found alone. It is, so to say,
the lower limit of the range of being. Always
it is joined with some form. So with the inorganic things of nature. But now notice that
the act-potency relation is not symmetrical.
Act is higher than potency: it is the active
agent over against mere passive capacity. It
has more of being in it: a fuller degree of
reality. If this relationship is generally characteristic of the real world, we may then expect
to find, so to speak, different levels of being.
And they will have to one another the act–
potency relation. Observation confirms the
suggestion. We find that the substances of
the inorganic realm have the capacity of taking on the properties of life. Plants manu-
facture their material out of the inorganic
elements, carbon, hydrogen, oxygen, nitro-
gen, etc. These are the potency of plant life.
The informing principle of plant life—its
substantial form—is just the active agency

shown in the green plants' energy of the
chlorophyll, circulation of sap, and so on.
Again, plants become food for animals. Plant
material is the source of animal food. All
animal life in the end is made from plants:
every animal, including man, is at bottom a
vegetarian. Thus plants are the potency of
animal life. The substantial form of the animal is the source of its activities and powers:
these are sensibility and appetition or desire.
With these appears consciousness. And these
functions in their turn are potencies in relation to man's conscious life. Man is distinguished from other animals by his reasoning power and his deliberate choice or
volition. But he could never reason or choose
unless he had sense-impressions to tell him
of the facts of nature and native desires to
give him something to choose from. Sensibility and desire are in a way the matter of
his intellectual and volitional life; they provide the possibility of these two. Intellect
and will are expressions of human substantial form: they are the specially human activities of rational thought and deliberate
conduct.

Well, we trace the thing out no further.

Enough to say that the spiritual world, which the scholastic accepts on purely rational grounds, is also explained to contain higher and higher levels of being, up to the Creator or First Cause of all below Him, He himself being pure act with no potency. But now notice an important consequence of this up-down, vertical stratification. If there is to be order, things must keep their places. If the colonel is higher than the captain, then the captain cannot issue the commands the colonel can issue. He must not exceed the limits of his position. And these limits must be well defined. So it is in nature. A plant has the power of growth and feeding and reproduction, but it has not the powers of sensation, memory, or desire. An animal can see and remember, but it cannot form abstract ideas or reason by propositions. And so on. Each is confined within barriers which it cannot pass. Within these barriers there is any amount of variation: the numerous animal genera and species, plant genera and species, etc. Also within them is any amount of change. And this is as true of individuals as of species. Each individual man has his essence, his substantial form as a human being; this he cannot exceed, though he manifests it in many different ways, as a banker, a cardplayer, a husband, a father, and in the minor activities of his life that vary from hour to hour and day to day. Each man, animal, plant, chemical molecule, atom has its fixed entelechy: it can never pass over into another one. It may change all you please within the limits prescribed; it may be destroyed as a plant is killed or water broken down into H_2 and O, but it cannot transgress the fixed boundaries of its nature. With order go rigid fixed limits.

The picture here drawn of scholasticism is scanty in the extreme, doubtless unjust in many ways. It is practically impossible to convey in so few words a proper sense of the care in detail, the wealth of argument, the breadth of view that have gone to the making of this system. It is far and away the greatest achievement in the past history of philosophy. All we have tried to do here is to bring out a certain note which seems central or pivotal, the note of the hierarchic order, the structural emphasis of the system, the fixed levels of being, containing much change and variety within each level, yet never overlapping, never exceeding the limits assigned to each within the general order.

For it is just this note of fixity that brings out the contrast between this great type of thought and the polar opposite type, modern process-philosophy. The key notion of the latter, as we are later to see, is precisely the denial of rigid limits in the order of nature. Evolution means the passing of limits—from the flagellates all the way up to man. The process of nature knows no final, ultimate barriers. Dogs may not now reason as men do, but in the course of future evolution who knows what new variation may not lead them into the domain of rational thought? And so on. But we do not here set out this new type of philosophy: that shall come later; for by its novelty it deserves, and needs, a chapter to itself.

So far we have before us four types, with a schism within one of them. See how they arrange themselves. We have three pairs of opposites: mind and body, one and many, fixed structure and process. Polar opposites we call them because in each couple the one member is the specific counterpart of the other: the two belong together. There is no counterpart relation between mind and process, or many and structure. Opposites we call them because it seems so natural to find them mutually exclusive. Who can believe that if John Jones is one person he is also two persons? That if God is one, He is also more than one? Who can persuade himself that ultimate reality may be of several kinds? We have a monistic bias. The ultimate must be definite, uncompromising, this or that and nothing else. If it is mind, it cannot be body; if it is permanent, it cannot change; if it is a fixed order, how could it possibly be an evolving growing affair? Well, if we are talking of ultimates, this is our ultimate situation in philosophy. It was always so, more or less; it still is so, and more rather than less. Beneath all minor criticisms and refutations lie these three deep rifts.

The situation is very dark, very hopeless. And from it comes that last pair of types named above, rationalism and irrationalism. The rationalist believes there is a way out even if we haven't yet found it. The irrationalist, grounding on the hopelessness of agreement, affirms that metaphysics is an impossible quest. We cannot understand reality, we cannot draw a map that can be proved correct, we cannot demonstrate ultimate truth. Reality is unintelligible, even meaningless. Of course this conclusion is repugnant to a healthy-minded human nature. For every man who is more than an animal mechanism repeating day by day the same routine—eating, drinking, turning a crank, pressing buttons, drawing pay—any such man has some general notion of the environment and what he can do with it, and so far a metaphysic. So men are normally not content to stop with the thesis of unintelligibility; accepting the external world, they assert some other means of getting acquainted with it, and replace intellect by sensation, or aesthetic intuition, or even mystical experience. These are the positive forms of irrationalism: the negative or extreme form is scepticism. Scepticism is the philosophy of despair; it hasn't the heart to seek new solutions for old difficulties.

In the sequel we shall not explicitly discuss these two types; we shall urge that the ground of irrationalism is quite false, since the other types do not need to disagree. For the rest we shall admit that irrationalism is right so far as it is positive and points to some additional way of reaching reality besides observation and reasoning. Evidence for this will be given in Chapter II.

The issue really turns on the above three pairs.

Now to repeat a much needed caution: Let not our attention be diverted from this situation by the criticism that our terms are so lacking in precision, so vague and loose as to rob the argument of meaning. The objection is irrelevant. Precise notions are not always significant notions. Who has a precise idea of death, or of life? But we certainly make some important use of these concepts. So here. We do not firmly outline the above nodes of thought: the shots at them by thinkers group themselves rather irregularly about them—yet we apprehend the groups well enough for our purpose.

But one might ask: why just *these* groups? True, the names are old: but might not a different classification be truer? We might have said voluntarism, intellectualism, phenomenology, determinism, realism, or what not. Of course; but we see at once that these latter are not significant or fertile enough to

raise fundamental lasting cleavages. They
have not enough practical bearing; and after
all a true philosophy must be a livable one.
The mind–body issue we can't help taking
pretty seriously. Immortality, morality, religion—these *matter*: and a materialist, if
consistent, gives a profoundly different answer to their problems from the idealist answer. The very words of common life point
the claim. Religion *matters*, the choice of
one's morality *matters*. Equally we say: I do
not *mind*, or I *mind* a great deal. The two
words connote serious concern, significance.
They have more import than most pairs.
Take also the order–process couple. The
terms embody the conservative–radical split
in politics, social life, morals, science, art—
in everything. What is there more meaningful than this? What causes more bloodshed
today? Of old it was the mind–body conflict,
witnessed in the quarrels about religion; today it is the order–process conflict, witnessed
in the fighting ideologies; the philosophical
rift goes with a rift in the plan of life. No:
look at the types of philosophy, not as so
many speculative possibilities, but as charts
of reality drawn by man as guides to life's

voyage—and you will see the inevitableness of the above polar opposites, their supreme importance.

How then in the face of this perennial conflict, quite as strong as ever today, can we go on trying to construct a good chart? Could anything be more hopeless, more a waste of precious time and energy?

But now a tiny ray of light appears.

The fighting couples we have called polars. They are not just blind oppositions. The terms *belong* together. Obvious suggestion: both are true of reality, but in different perspective, perhaps—or something like that. But we must first have evidence that both *are* true and real.

Isn't it very probable that a view which has survived some three thousand years among the most intelligent class of man— surely philosophers have been such—has a deal of truth? So much smoke, some fire. If men can't help believing something, isn't it at least very very plausible? Survival value, let us call it. Would a belief survive as long as we have records of sincere careful thinking, unless it had a truth value? So we strongly feel. Of course this does not give that certainty, that absolute assurance, which is the philosopher's quest. He, unlike other men who are content with the day-by-day practical assurance that is enough for them, wants some eternally unassailable security. You and I are not absolutely certain that the sun will rise tomorrow; yet we don't worry about it because we are occupied with preparing for it; but the philosopher craves an absolute assurance—perhaps not about the sun rising, but about the fundamentals that man so dearly loves. Still, is there not a pretty good chance that he has touched these, in this perennial recurrence of conviction?

The argument is suggestive and hopeful. But think, on the other hand, how many convictions have survived through the ages that we cannot consider even respectable. Many many people still believe in omens, magic, charms, etc. These we cannot take seriously. They aren't the intelligent people. But consider the expert philosophers. They believe most devoutly that the types disagree and must disagree. Each member of a type believes, and has perennially believed, that if his type is right the others must be wrong. The survival-argument contradicts itself.

The belief in each type has persisted; so also has the belief of each type that it only is right equally persisted. We get no conclusion from persistence.

But these considerations are too subjective, too narrowly human. We have not asked about evidence. Is there evidence in favor of each type? Is there evidence of their mutual exclusion? The moment we consider the situation in this impersonal objective way, it appears on an entirely different footing. For there *is* evidence that each type is right in what it positively affirms, and there is *no* evidence that each type is right in excluding the other types. Consider this evidence. The idealist claims that mind is real. No doubt he is right. Nobody denies that there are such things as minds, or such processes as mental processes. Everybody *verifies*, or can verify, the existence of minds. None of us could live a single day without admitting that he and his fellows think, feel, and will. The reality of the thing or process we call mind is verified beyond question. So too is the materialist's claim for the reality of physical things and processes. The sun, stars, planets, hills, woods, waters, these are daily verified beyond a doubt. We all actually accept these as undeniable facts. And so, once more of the scholastic view of the levels of being. Atoms, molecules, plants, animals, man—these are well verified, and their difference in grade or richness of being is equally well verified. No one questions that a man has more in him than an arthropod or a coelenterate, or that a plant is more complex than a molecule of H_2O. And the fact of process and change, too, no one denies. All these positive claims of the types have sufficient evidence. Each type undeniably points to certain real things in the world. But now we ask: does each type verify the inconsistency of his view with the other views? Does any one prove by incontestable *evidence* that what is mind cannot also be material, and so on? We answer: quite the contrary. As far as appeal to admitted facts goes, the evidence is all the other way. An individual person is *both* mind and body. So far as concrete experience tells us, what is mind is *also* body—in the case of man and the higher animals. The two seem integrally united in one. Again, so far as we have evidence, everything that is one is *also* many. A rose, a stone, a man, is one individual and no other, but it is very complex. Even a man is the seat of opposing impulses. Nothing is merely one or merely many. And do we know of any fixed species that do not give birth to species just a bit different, with new mutations perhaps that in time give new species? Biologists tell us that species is a very relative term. No, so far as convincing evidence goes, we never find a simon-pure exclusion between the types. Rather we find the claims of each confirmed together. The one thing that is *never* verified is their mutual exclusion.

Evidently there is some other motive at work that dictates this exclusion—and with it the hopeless situation above set forth. It is presumably some ultimate test we have at the back of our minds, some criterion of what reality must be, and what it cannot be. We feel that even if *in fact* mind and body are often joined in one, if *in fact* permanent things change, and so on, somehow reason dictates that such facts are not truly real. What then is this criterion that reason lays down? What anyway should be our criterion of reality? Until this question is decided, we cannot judge about the mutual consistency of the types, or indeed about the ultimate truth of any one type. Nor can we see how the process-type might suggest a resolution of the quarrels, unless we see it in accord with a just criterion.

The search for the criterion must be our next topic.

II

THE CRITERION OF REALITY

PHILOSOPHY appears to the outsider, and to the beginning student, a welter of conflicting systems. We have found that if we look at this welter in a nonpartisan way, it reveals an order beneath the surface confusion. The systems fall into types: like plants and animals, they show a natural classification. And what is more we have found something like a typical relation between them—the relation of polar opposition. There is materialism and its specific opposite idealism. There is scholasticism and its specific opposite process-philosophy. There is monism and its specific opposite pluralism. We have said *specific* three times, to emphasize that these pairs are *natural* pairs: the two members of each belong to each other. So the situation clears itself up a little; the confusion is not so great as to render a choice of system quite impossible or quite arbitrary.

Still the opposition remains. Each type earnestly refutes all the others. If we are to choose between them, then, obviously we must have some well-grounded criterion. A

criterion of what? Well, since all these systems profess to state what is real, ultimately
real, not just a temporary appearance but the
very essence of the world about us—it really
is mind, though it doesn't always look so, it
really is bodies in motion, though we men
seem to be partly mind and not body—since
all the quest is of reality, we naturally need
some mark or test of reality. How are we
to discriminate this genuinely real of the
philosopher from the apparently real things?
And presumably each of the type-systems
has at the back of its head some such criterion
which it doesn't always bring into the open:
presumably, too, the criteria differ, since the
results differ. Then certainly we must be
clear as to what is the right criterion.

All the more is this needed for our present
task. We are going to claim that the latest-
born of these types—process-metaphysic—
has a point of view which enables us to har-
monize the oppositions. Plainly then we
must be very confident of *its* criterion.

We shall use the method of trying one
after another, the criteria that have been
proposed or might be proposed, to see if
they suffice. Let us hope our list is complete.

Presentedness

Begin with a very simple one: the real is
that which is just presented or given. Illusion
is that which is not given, but assumed, in-
vented. Stones, trees, houses are presentations; mermaids are not. How do I know
that the tree is real? Because I see it. Seeing
is believing. But suppose the light is dim;
night is coming on. Then perhaps I wait till
tomorrow when I clearly see it. Clearly?
Then it is not just the seeing, but the *clear*
seeing, that counts. We recall Descartes'
phrase "clear and distinct." What is clear
and distinct to thought is true. So what is
clear and distinct to vision is real. And the
like of hearing and other senses; though in
none does the clearness or distinctness usually reach the degree attained in vision.
Which perhaps is why vision is felt to be *the*
reality-sense. But a little reflection shows
that the phrase "clear and distinct vision"
contains a tautology. The adjectives add
nothing; we might just as well say vision
alone. What is dimly and confusedly seen is,
so far as the content of the object is concerned, not seen. It is dark on the water; I

cannot distinguish the horizon; only an in-
distinct difference of the light suggests where
it may lie. I don't *see* the horizon. Obviously,
the degree of clear-distinct is strictly correlative to degree of information received in
vision. The more clearly I see, the more
things I see. So our criterion returns to its
initial simplicity. Seeing is believing. We
see the reality; its evidence is sufficient by
itself. Listen to this:

I could scarcely persuade myself that the whole
affair was not a dream—that the men who sat
all round us in little groups, the dark liveried
servants passing noiselessly backwards and for-
wards, were not figures in some shadowy nightmare, and that I should not wake in a moment to
find myself curled up in a railway carriage on my
way home. But there was no mistaking the
visible presence of Colonel Mostyn Ray. Strong,
stalwart, he sat within a few feet of me. . . . He,
at least, was real.[1]

This is thoroughly characteristic of the presentation test. Why, how, by what standard
was he real? "No mistaking the visible presence"—the statement is absolute, ground-
less, authoritative. But it is of the nature of

1. E. Phillips Oppenheim, *The Betrayal*, p. 163. By permission of Little, Brown, and Company.

authority to abolish tests. Mere vision, then, would be just plain acceptance of the given *without* a test. It sets rather than settles the problem.

And in fact, we don't always seem to accept vision, even clear and distinct vision, as the test. Many are the optical illusions of size, distance, etc. The illusion, for instance, of the Zöllner lines, is visually quite clear-cut. There is as little obscurity and confusion in the sight of a straight stick out of water as of a bent stick half in the water. Is vision then not sufficient? But see how we correct it: by more vision. We measure the lines and angles of the Zöllner figure *looking at* the marks on the ruler; we take the bent stick out of the water, or immerse it wholly, and *look at it*. Incidentally, too, we may call in touch—not usually so well accredited, because of its lesser definiteness. But the principle is this: as we cure the ills of democracy by more democracy, we cure the illusions of perception by more perception. Again we return to the simple authoritative pronouncement: presentation is the ultimate test. Authority once more. But we cannot help asking, why this authority, not some other?

Self-Evidence

Vision is very convincing, no doubt; but what certainty have we that we see rightly? The trouble is that sense experience is confined to present time, and how do we know that soon some new vision may not deny what we now see? How do we know that we shan't wake up? We want a criterion that is not subject to accidents of time or place: something absolutely self-guaranteeing. Consider for example the truths of reason: the necessary truths of logic or mathematics. We cannot doubt $2 + 3 = 5$; we cannot deny the law of identity or of contradiction, or the principle of sufficient reason. We cannot doubt *A implies B, B implies C, therefore A implies C*. Truths like these are a last court of appeal. We try to deny them, we try to imagine them false, as we *can* imagine our vision of sun and moon false, but we cannot do it. They are undeniable; they cannot be proved, but they are the basis of all proof. There is something about their content and meaning that forces conviction. In short, they are self-evident; they are presentations that prove themselves. Now, it is suggested, reality is like that. It is a necessary presupposition of thinking. There *must* be reality. It is a logical implication, self-evident.

Unless there were an external reality, there would be no object for thinking, nothing for us to understand, puzzle over, etc. There must be an object, else there would be no subject, as the two terms are correlative. Descartes, who is largely responsible for our whole problem, made the initial error of separating subject and object, whereas they are always together. But who does not see that this criticism of Descartes is only another way of affirming that subject implies object? In the end it is always the binding claim that we come back to: ". . . spontaneous and even irresistible assent."[2] It is the position of common sense, but common sense reflected upon, codified, and justified as a necessary implication of thought.

All right: let us grant a self-evident implication that there must be reality of some sort. Let us admit that we could not even doubt that so and so is real, if we did not have some

2. Cardinal Désiré Joseph Mercier, *A Manual of Modern Scholastic Philosophy* (1st English ed. London, Kegan Paul, Trench, Trubner, 1916), I, 350.

notion of what reality means, of what would
be a criterion of reality. But this general ad-
mission furnishes no clue whatever to any
specific criterion. It gives no limit of *what*
conditions must be fulfilled, if some presentation or other is to be real. It is just too
general, too abstract, to be of any use. We
might just as well go back to vision, or hearing, or smelling, to find out what presentations are real. No specific test has appeared.

Intuition or Mystical Experience

The proposed criterion of necessary implication, then, gives no inkling of what is
real, what only illusion or imagination. It is
too general. Let us then seek for some test
which will discriminate between presentations and yet go deeper than the mere just-
now-given which might later be denied:
some test, that is, other than the sense-per-
ception of the moment, such as vision. For
instance, take intuition as defended by Bergson, or mystical contact with the divine, the
latter considered by many devout souls and
through the ages as the supreme warrant of
reality. Perhaps other sorts too should be

named. But we see at once that this resort to a special *kind* of presentation, no matter what be the kind, leaves us just where we were, without a test. Consider intuition. It is not necessary for our purpose to get a precise Bergsonian definition of this term (what in so artistic a stylist would be well-nigh impossible anyway). Enough that it is a special way of insight into the processes of life, other than conceptual knowledge, probably other than sensation. It claims the unique privilege of getting reality; the other sources distort by one-sidedness, selection due to practical interest, abstraction of a part from the living whole. For example—the only Bergsonian example we have found—we intuit the passage of time in our own conscious life. Note now that the reason for preferring intuition is that it does *not* cut up the presented flowing continuum into discrete parts—which would be an artificial construction. Intuition gives the fact direct, without interference by the beholder. It is, after all, just simple presentation again. A kind of presentation is fixed on because it is a simon-pure kind, which means unqualified presentation, no special kind at all in fact. We are

back where we were: we have but a purer
form of presentation.

But what of mystical vision? (Above we
said contact; here intentionally vision; both
are of course analogues, and given to suggest the impossibility of precise definition.)
Its full import for knowledge we cannot here
take up. But this much can be said now: it is
the object, the divine being, which renders
the experience unique. The mystical insight
is not made by some particular faculty or
function, comparable to eye or ear. Call it an
intense and burning sense of the presence of
God; but this sense is not some privileged
organ of man's mind which is superior to
other organs in having exclusive access to
reality. There is no identifiable mystical
organ. It is, after all, just presentation, even
though the object presented is, like the sun
to the human eye, so overwhelming and
dazzling as to forbid doubt and to influence
deeply the mystic's life. There is here, in
fact, no special kind of presentedness, to be
taken as unique dative quality or criterion of
reality. We have only a very concentrated
presentedness. Again we are back where we
started: presentation in general, a genus

without a species, without the means of discrimination between one datum and another. And we can see that any ground of discrimination rests its claim only on the assumption that it gives the purest and cleanest instance of presentedness.

So the notion of some special *kind* of presentation as a criterion will have to be given up. We find no such kind. But already from the mystical experience has emerged a new notion: degree. Presentations differ in degree of presentedness; not in the clear distinct way which refers only to the number of things presented, but in the impressiveness of what we just now called dative quality. This intensive difference is what is called strength, vividness, vivacity, or force. The sun overhead on a hot midsummer day seems inescapably real. The din of an explosion presses its reality into the hearer's consciousness; he cannot doubt it. Recall Hume's distinction between impressions and ideas; Locke's between ideas of sensation and ideas of reflection. The distinction is an old one; perhaps we shall find here a good criterion.

Degree or Force of Presentation

The presentations of waking life are typically stronger than those of dream life, or those of memory and reverie. That, we are now told, is why we believe them to portray the real. Imagination is weak. We say to a man "you have a vivid imagination," meaning that his images are so vivid that he takes them as percepts; thereby we acknowledge the present criterion. And there is no denying the *general* fact of correlation.

But of course there are exceptions. Some dreams are very vivid; more so than some waking experiences. The hallucinations of delirium tremens are probably more vivid than many normal perceptions of the external world. Certainly some visual illusions are quite as strongly felt as correctly seen objects. The two lines of the familiar Müller-Lyer illusion look just as vividly of different length after the arrowheads are added as they looked equal before: neither impression is more forcible than the other.

And the test is so vague. How much strength must a presentation have to be a genuine percept? We can draw no line, however thick: there are not even assignable limits below or above which a datum is certainly imaginary or real and between which it is doubtful. My hearing of the street noises while I write is certainly less vivid than the lively dream I had last night of conversing with a friend long since dead.

But would the test of force, however vague it be, have so general an application unless somehow sound? Difficult to apply it may be; insufficient it may be. Yet there is a naturalness about it. It is more specific than the general logical implication that there must be reality somewhere, and it seems to mean more than mere presentedness. Obviously, the point lies in the stronger compulsion. A stronger datum is harder to doubt; it compels belief more. This motive of power is a new note; it looks like a definite quality giving a kind of solid core to the datum. This much then we may retain from the present criterion; reality has an objective element of compulsion, and thus perhaps a certain relation to the will or action of the beholder. At least it controls his attention, and attention is usually some degree of action. We shall later make use of this.

Nevertheless, the present test if regarded as a mode of presentation is altogether too unworkable. Beyond the statement that typically, or under normal conditions, what is real in the external world is more vivid than what is imaginary, we can make no use of it; for we have no line marking out the degree requisite for reality. Except for the note of relation to our own activity, we have just presentedness again, though more of it as in mystical experience.

Relation of Presentations: Coherence

We have been dealing above with presentations in isolation. We spoke of *a* visual datum, *a* sound, *an* intuition, etc., quite without regard to its connection with others. Was that not an error? Surely we experience no presentations alone. Idealists tell us that there are no single sense-data apart from the thoughts that connect, relate and interpret them; that a mere "brute" datum is meaningless. No wonder we failed to find a criterion; we went about it the wrong way. Our method was false to the facts. Presentations hang together.

See now how this throws light on our problem.

We all believe that the world of everyday presentations is real, while the world of dreams is not. Why? Because the former is, on the whole, one big consistent presentation, while the latter contains separate presentations that contradict one another and contradict those of our waking life. The streets and houses, the sun and moon, the trees, and even the persons of daily experience are more or less the same from day to day, and their variations do not interfere with their continued identity. Apart from some puzzles—a friend acts in an unaccustomed way, an exceptionally violent storm or an earthquake upsets the usual course of things—the whole scene hangs together. As philosophers say, it is coherent. The collection of our dreams does not, in respect of its presentations (sometimes very clear and vivid), fit together: there is little coherence. One night I dream I am in Antarctica, the next night in the tropics; one night I converse with a friend long dead, the next with a centaur; even within one dream, a person I know suddenly loses his identity, turns into someone else. So of course we believe in the reality of the former, not of the latter.

This looks like a new and good criterion: it is made central by one of the types of metaphysic (idealism). For it seems to contain a ground, a reason for accrediting some presentations over others. *Mere* presentedness, as we saw, is a mystery; it has no way of discriminating, no test between reality and illusion. But coherence adds a test; only the presentations that hang together in an order are accredited as real.

Let us examine its credentials. Why does it commend itself so readily? Because it gives to each presentation a firmness and a maintenance which would otherwise be lacking. United we stand, divided we fall: each helps to maintain the other. Yesterday the table in my new office was observed by me as brown; today the like is observed, and so on. Each observed datum gets an added security from each predecessor and each successor. Think of a ninepin standing on the floor which if alone might be easily knocked over but when supported by a closely packed surrounding group of ninepins stands very firm. What they give to the lone ninepin by their added support is, however, not some new and irreducible quality; it is only more of what it possessed before—more standing, so to say. So too when presentations imply, cohere with, support one another; the added relation gives no new mysterious quality, *existence*, not had before. It gives only more *presentation*, a stronger maintenance of the presentedness. In the end the test is presentation and more presentation. If the single presentation were, like an immovable ninepin, so firm and strong that it could not be removed, then indeed no coherence-test would be needed. Stable presentation is what we have got. It is the mental world of epistemological idealism. Once more we are back where we were; only we have now dug ourselves in, so to speak. Well, says the idealist, is not that all that reality means? We say no; there is another note, and indeed the primary note. And no presentational test alone can give it. Consider an example.

A literary genius writes a novel, poem, or drama. It is a long, complex affair—a *Paradise Lost*, a *Divine Comedy*, a *Hamlet* on a scale so large that the writer takes (say) fifty years to complete it; the book itself runs

to (say) twenty large volumes. Let us suppose that there is a coherence of the characters and events well-nigh impeccable: all
hang together as in the most perfect work
of art. Would the reader then take it for a
large slice of reality? An excerpt from history perhaps? Not to the slightest degree.
However massive the content and thorough
the interpenetration, there would be no least
inclination to accept the world of the drama
as even a separate reality, apart from the
physical world. The example is made to have
enormous spread, precisely because it shows
that *amount* of hanging together has no bearing upon existence. The reader of so huge a
work would not be more inclined to see it
real than if the work had only one hundred
pages and three characters. Yet the characters and events do support one another, so
to speak, a great deal more in the longer
work.

The insufficiency of the coherence-test
may be seen in another way. As far as our
human experience goes, it is not absolutely
coherent. We say the outer world is so, and
the dream world is not so: but the difference
is only of degree, however great. There are

plenty of things and events in the external world that we have not succeeded in fitting into a total order of nature. In the earlier days of science, it looked as if we had. The Newtonian physics seemed to be such a wholly ordered scheme; and it was in those days that the Kantian-Hegelian idea of reality as a completely coherent, organized system arose. But the physics of today has shown us that we have not got any such system in our possession. We have not yet wholly succeeded in seeing how the quantum-phenomena fit in with wave-phenomena; or whether electrons, protons, etc., are wave-systems or bodies or both, or whether gravitation can be brought under the theory of relativity. Much of the external world, in short, remains incoherent to us. And on the other hand much of the unreal world of dreams has some degree of coherence. Some dreams are fairly coherent; and the daydreams that become embodied in beautiful works of art are usually, if not always, very coherent. Do you object that even if coherent within, they do not fit in with the vastly more coherent world of our everyday observation, the external physical world?

True, they do not; but where are we to draw the line between the amount of coherence needed to give reality and the amount that is not sufficient? It appears that the question would have to be decided by majority vote. The more votes a presentation can get—the more implications it can draw from other presentations—the more chance it has of being real. But here is no *guarantee* of its reality.

As a matter of fact, what the idealists do is to assume a real external world at the beginning and then go on to argue that it *must* be coherent, that coherence gives it the title to reality. But they have never demonstrated any one quite coherent body of presentations, and accordingly have never presented us with any genuine reality. True, they argue that such reality is a postulate of thought, a presupposition of reason, etc. This appeal to the criterion of logical necessity we have dealt with above. It shows only that there must be a reality of some sort somewhere, but it gives us no test for discovering that reality in any particular presentations.

It comes down to this: unless you have a *workable* criterion for deciding *between* pres-

entations—the idealist test being not workable—you have no sufficient criterion of reality. Presentation needs an *external* test;
coherence is not such; it means only firmer,
stronger presentation, a matter of degree.
So we are prodded along to seek some new
criterion, foreign to the categories of the
presentational point of view.

Where shall we look for it? The presentational point of view is that of contemplation, still awareness. In vision, which is its
sensuous representative, action is at a minimum: even more so in the flashlight intuition
of logical relations by intellect. The contrast
appears between thought and action. The
other great aspect of our experience, counterpart of the cognitive, claims our notice: the
practical, wherein we act.

Our acts are directed primarily toward the
obtaining of goods—life, health, prosperity,
friends, and so on, and the avoiding of evils—
death, sickness, poverty, enmity, and so on.
Here is the realm of values, as the cognitive
is the realm of truths. Not that this realm
and the cognitive do not interpenetrate: obviously they do. But that does not remove a
deep difference of emphasis. And it would be

strange indeed if the meaning of reality to us men were unconnected with *both* sides of our lives; if reality which comes to us in the guise and disguise of presentation for contemplation, did not also come to us as source of the good we seek and the evil we avoid. But if it does the latter, it will be revealed, not primarily by the tests of logic known to the cultivated thinker alone, but by tests used in the daily life of uncultivated as well as cultivated man. For all alike seek goods and shun evils. The meaning and test of reality in the practical sphere will then be discovered in everyday human action. We shall ask, not what *ought* reality to mean to intellect, but what *does* it mean to the common man in his working life, and how does he come to believe in a real over against an imaginary world?

Yet before tracing out this new criterion, we must say this. We have found the contemplative tests insufficient: we have not found them erroneous. Surely we must have presentations in order to know reality; surely they must be coherent if they hold of reality. Surely then, the proper test, whatever it be, will find a place for the above criteria. The claim will in fact be made that they are necessary but not sufficient conditions of reality.

The Practical Test

A normal man untainted by epistemology believes that the objects he sees in ordinary waking life are real in themselves, other than his own mind, other than the sensations or the inferences he entertains, and independent of his knowing them. Why? Because when he tries to do something to them he finds them resisting (at least somewhat) and showing a power of their own. Given a heavy stone, he tries to lift it; it requires some muscular effort, more perhaps than he thought. He has to adapt his conduct to its weight: the weight so far exerts power over his conduct, resists encroachment with a power of its own. He tries to crush it with his fingers—it is too hard. He can't do anything with it he might wish. The same is true of any real object. The object in fact is real, not imaginary, just because it "speaks up for itself," shows control over his acts: limited control of course, yet enough always to modify his acts. He sees a tree and reaches out to touch it; but he cannot touch it unless he first walks forward a few paces; then he does touch it. Distance thus becomes externally real to him; he has to adapt his conduct to it. He goes to the railroad station to take a train; he cannot board the train because he is too early, and must wait till it arrives at twelve o'clock. He is obliged to adapt his conduct to time; time thus becomes an external reality, because it has power over him. He finds by acting and experimenting that wood floats and iron sinks, that a gas balloon rises, that electricity passes through copper wire, that energy is conserved, that nature's power takes the form of laws, and so on. Nature comes to have reality because he has to take account of it in what he tries to do. That is the great lesson of the experimental method; try to do something with things and you will find out what they *really* are. Passive observation would never discover the secrets of nature— what nature *really* is of itself. A merely visualizing animal, if there could be one, would have little or no sense of a world outside itself. The natural sciences teach a vast *respect* for nature.

But man believes in a world which is more than physical. He believes in other minds than his own. Instinct or analogy or what not suggests the notion of another mind early in his life; conduct more and more confirms it. For he finds that his conduct has to pay regard to them. He has to consider and respect motives, thoughts, feelings, etc., like his own, else he could not gain his ends. The social categories are requisites of his behavior.

Nay, we may go further. The man who genuinely believes in God, does so because certain of his experiences seem to him to show a spiritual force—a moral law, an impulse of universal benevolence, an ideal of justice—which he finds that he cannot disregard without grievous, even intolerable, inner torment. Apart from such power over conduct, religion is but academic. The word is significant: it denotes a separation of thought from the real world, as the young are segregated in a school. And we might almost endlessly illustrate the plain fact that men not sophisticated by self-conscious reflection do accept external reality of any sort—physical, mental, spiritual—because

they have learned that they must respect
forces greater than their own. All control is
won first by obedience; and obedience is to
something not ourselves.

The examples given are drawn from adult
life. A baby takes weeks, months, years to
learn from his attempted and frustrated ac-
tions that there is a world external to himself. True, one instance would be enough to
prove external reality, if only he were a clear
thinker; but grown men are seldom that,
still less infants. The concept of an external
world is a slow growth, and long experience
goes into its making. But it constantly gains
strength, as instance after instance occurs in
which he finds that he must adjust his conduct, if he would gain his ends, to powers
that dwell in the qualities, the things, relations, and events which are presented to his
consciousness. And when he is adult, the
conviction is so firmly fixed that it can
scarcely be dislodged.

Now, as noted above, the action-test may
not be the only one needed. But we can see
at once that there is a kind of primacy about
it. For it conveys the sense of externality, of
something over and above the realm of the

effort made; since the object in some measure overpowers that effort. What *overpowers*, is *over and above*, and so far independent,
external, something by itself and in itself.
This provides what we may call the reality-
coefficient of the datum. Of itself it gives
small information, though it does give some,
as to the character and make-up of that
which resists. If it be a stone that we try to
lift, the resistance tells us only that the stone
is heavy; if we try to dent the same with our
finger, we learn only that it is hard. Visual
qualities, tones, scents, etc., we do not seem
to get that way: perhaps only pressure and
muscular qualities. It is the existential aspect which is prominent in the action-test;
action tells chiefly *that* something is. And as
this existence is so directly encountered in
action—nothing could be more direct, simple, or immediate—we feel a bedrock foundation vouchsafed. The point is that the test
of action guarantees external reality; presentation offers the material and action reveals its existence. The theoretical tests
proposed above and found insufficient are
thus admitted as necessary; but they are
made valid, so to speak, given existential

significance, only by the practical test. As regards reality, the latter is primary, the former secondary, though both are needed.

But we must now examine carefully the claim just made. The view is no new one, but has seldom made much play in the type systems; the philosopher would, *ex professo*, incline to a purely logical criterion. Consequently its significance has seldom, if ever, been brought out.

Take again our simplest of examples: we push against a heavy rock, and find that it resists, overcomes, to a degree nullifies our effort. The resistance, directly felt, is the reaction or *power* of the rock. Power here means nothing hidden or inferred; it is immediately experienced in the overpowering of the effort. It is the *over* in overpowered that is the mark of externality: and externality means otherness. But—otherness to what? To an ego that puts forth the effort? Surely we have no right to take for granted such a late product of reflection in so simple an experience as a push of the arm.

Agreed. But we are not starting from the subjective realm. That would already imply contrast with the objective and beg reality at the start. The effort and the feeling of it, which we have assumed present, are no more than experiences, qualitatively unique, and proceeding in time. All that we are initially assuming is in one region—a continuum of experience, with no distinction of subjective versus objective; with no distinctions at all indeed but the numerical, relational, and qualitative ones inherent in any flux of events. Then we find one part of this flux (which we called the active effort) running up against some quality (the overpowering) which quality does at once divide the continuum into two parts—the act and the resisting datum external to and independent of the effort. The gray surface of the stone resists my push—the gray stone is real. But there is also the push; and here indeed is doubtless the origin of our consciousness of the subjective, of the self, and its functioning, etc. When the concept of the self does appear, it grows out of this primary and primitive sense of effort put forth. True enough, this notion of the self, like that of the external world, is a slow growth. The point is that, again like the notion of the outer reality, the locus of its growth, the growing tip of this tender plant, lies in the active experiences. The very center and essence of a self is its aims, desires, drives; so much have we learned from modern psychology. And these which are its efforts, become differentiated out, over against the environment, precisely through the oppositions that meet the efforts. And this experienced contrast widens and deepens with added experience, until it is rounded out into the full awareness of the distinction between self and external world.

So far as to the natural origin of our belief in external things and events as distinct from the subjective world of our efforts, aims, wants, and all the thoughts and fancies that go with them. But granting this *de facto*, is it *de jure*? Have we the *right* to claim from our experience of resisted action that there *is* a real external world?

When one thing or process opposes, blocks, or overpowers another, the two are so far distinct. Opposing currents in a river are traceable to distinct sources: the gravitation and the resisting rocks on the bottom, or the like. The opposing forces in a living body that make it sicken or die come from different organs, different chemicals, different trends in the cells, tissues, etc., or other separate factors. No one thing, so far as it is one, can destroy itself. This is the soundest logic, because it is tautology: a thing is itself and can't make itself be what isn't itself. And such logic is (natively and unconsciously) used when a man judges that what opposes his effort—himself, as he eventually feels, *is* his effort—is outside, existentially other than and independent of, himself. His judgment is not merely natural; it is inevitable, with the inevitableness and irrefutableness of a simple tautology. It is a true judgment.

The point is that so long as we act in order to gain our ends, we *cannot consistently avoid* using a category which is more than mere presentation: the category of a power not ourselves. And if not ourselves, then external to us. But action, and only action, gives us the right to this new category which we must call by the name of reality.

Note well that there is nothing of an a priori dictum here, no allegation of a presupposition of thought, no syllogizing, no inference or implication at all. There is sim-

ple, plain, direct experience. The resistance
is directly felt; there is no inferring an external cause of the resistance. "External" *means*
resisting: the cause is the felt power as it
performs the overpowering then and there.
There is no more direct and convincing
experience than this one of effort and opposition. We may go on to reason about the
further properties of the resisting thing; but
mere located resistance, as felt, is so far the
object itself. Nor is there the slightest
ground for calling this inevitable belief by
the sacred name of faith. Whatever faith
may mean (and it is well-nigh impossible to
tell what it does mean except for scholasticism) it certainly is not applicable to this
situation. For certainly no one would call it
a matter of faith to assert that he was seeing
a patch of blue color at the moment. The
present case is just like that. The felt resistance is no *messenger from* an external realm:
it *is* that realm. The externality is by resistance as straightly and indubitably given as
is the blue quality to the eye which senses it.
Externality, we may say, is for active effort
a sensed quality. We do not have to ask
whether externality is external. There is no

room for faith. Knowledge fills the place. We touch the external world as directly as our hands touch the wall they press.

Why then, you will ask, do we go to vision so much more than to touch, for evidence of physical things? What of the astronomer? How should he touch his stars and spiral nebulae? Along this line innumerable instances might be raised.

The answer is simple. In early life we *did* verify things mostly by touch, movement, manipulation. It was that that lodged our conviction of the external world. But we learned also that certain visual signs go with a fair certainty of verifiability in action. I see a house fifty feet away and have learned by many, many experiences that such an appearance practically always is confirmable by the active test. I *can* go up to it and feel the physical force of its mass and cohesion by pushing, etc. Normally, a man's vision, still more the vision of many, is a certain enough indication of reality. And most of us learned the action-test of reality so long ago that we have quite forgotten it. Dealing so much with distant objects as do the higher animals and man, they have developed the short-cut path to reality, of vision, and seldom resort to the laborious task, often the impossible task, of active contact. Vision is the staff of the scientific life, but resisted action is the solid ground on which the staff rests.

But is there not a kind of immediate revelation of objective existence quite apart from action, in certain sharp and shocking experiences, with no sense of resistance about them? A sudden harsh noise, such as the motor horn of today gives, wakes us out of a doze: there is a violent intrusion, something I would not have created if I could, something too repulsive for me to have conjured up. Or an unexpected thump on the back startles us when quietly reading; even the painful cinder that flies into the eye has its message of externality. Notice, however, that these cases have something in common. They go against the grain, they *break into* the smoothly going current of the moment. In fact they do most obviously display power by *overcoming* the easy flow of our experience. Yet even that flow is in some degree an active tendency. Yes; these cases do conform to the practical test.

But now we take a further step, already mentioned but not considered. And this is where we go beyond the present-day instrumentalism that lies so near to the above view. For we must declare that the resisting object is logically (and often temporally) independent of or antecedent to, the felt effort. Yes, our thesis will be the paradoxical assertion that the object is *perceived* by the acting subject as existing *independent of the perception.* Paradoxical of course this seems; but only because the modern epistemologist has become so concentrated upon the study of knowing, thinking, perception, etc., that he finds it hard to imagine or conceive a situation in which he is not there thinking it. He has retreated so far away from external nature and sunk so deep into his own mind, that he can hardly admit the possibility of the latter being absent. He even tends to take mind as a positive factor determining the object—whether in the timeless Kantian way or in the flowing manner of the instrumentalist. How get away from these consequences of the introvert epistemological attitude? We might here recall certain analogies from external nature herself. Light is not visible—i.e., not light—until it strikes an object; steam is not apparent until it becomes condensed into waterdrops; the eye sees the object without knowing itself present at all. For the eye to enter its own experience, another eye would be required to see it. Poetically and truly expressed, the eye is the transparent window of the soul, itself so transparent as to be vanishing. Aquinas in this connection used the example of a mirror, so clear as to be invisible. The point is that in the active experience, mind becomes transparent and self-effacing; present only potentially so to speak, but not actually present as component of the experience. Aristotle said that when we know, the mind in a way *becomes* the object, disappears into it. The object is there alone. After all, the view is an old one.

It is only by carrying over certain traits of material being to the region of mind that we find it paradoxical for mind to go out of itself. Space and time are exclusive; now is not then, here is not there. One body cannot efface itself, and become another individual body. All are self-enclosed. But mind is patently *not* self-enclosed. As perception, it grows by identifying itself with other things than itself; or with their accidental forms, as the scholastics say. It *humbles* itself, effaces itself, receiving its content from without. That is its normal procedure. The epistemologist, studying his own instrument thought, naturally reveres the object of his study: he thinks that mind must maintain itself, like a strong man, by its own power. Hence he can, as a rule, hardly bear to think of mind as self-effacing in true knowledge. He confuses humility with humiliation. He forgets that who would command must first obey. "Except a corn of wheat fall into the ground and die, it abideth alone; but if it die, it bringeth forth much fruit." These words apply to mind, which loses its being in the object and is resurrected in the knowledge it thereby gains and can use. Mind dies in order to live. But so far we have been talking only of the possibility, the nonparadoxical quality of the known being independent of the knower. Now to see how it applies in the present case of resisted effort.

At first sight the application looks too easy. What is sensed or otherwise experienced as *more than*, as *over*powering the ef-

fort, surely is sensed as *beyond* or *exceeding*
the effort; and surely what *exceeds* has something not due to, and therefore independent
of, that which it exceeds. The greater power
has elements of its own, not possessed by
nor derived from the lesser. The resisting
power of the heavy stone is derived wholly
from the stone, not from my effort. More-
over, it is *sensed as not affected* by the effort,
for it overcomes the effort. Common sense
feels that way: a man finding a stone too
heavy for him to lift would laugh if told that
the weight of the stone was dependent on
his effort. The practical experience, experience of power as it is, acknowledges that the
greater power is independent of the less.

But now the epistemologist brings up his
objections. He says that the man was after
all *experiencing* the independence of the too-
heavy stone; he can't get away from experience—that is the paradox above noted. How
then does the action-experience meet it? We
answer: in the same way as the eye sees an
object without contributing anything itself.
Let us here consider an example. A man is
standing on the crumbling edge of a sand-
stone cliff; he slips, begins to slide down-

ward, grasps frantically at the twigs, grass-blades, projecting stones. In that moment of intense action self-awareness ceases; the objects alone occupy the stage. True, the penumbra which surrounds that moment contains the felt effort, the fear, the imminent fall; but just so far as there is active concern with the means of safety, so far there is *given* an object pure and simple, and the *experience*-side has vanished. We say, looking back reflectively, "it was a harrowing experience": so for the cognitive consciousness which later views the total situation. But in the vivid moment of struggle for a handhold, consciousness melts into the objects. Those loose stones, that red sand, those twigs—they are not being experienced, *they are there*. The white heat of action melts consciousness into the object.

Here is the pertinence of the analogy with vision. Mind has this peculiar property, that it can go out of itself, sink into the object, and lose itself in that object. No material body can do this. In reflective thinking, to be sure, mind is the less likely to do so: there are too many suggestions, implications, associations that stand between it and its object. In this respect sense-knowledge, knowledge of the qualities of the external world, is more certain than reflective knowledge. *Men* agree about the one, and *philosophers* disagree about the other. But of course the analogy must not be pressed too hard. We are supposing an ideal case of vision with a real external world assumed, and after all our thesis does not find such a world guaranteed by vision, but by active behavior. But once grant such a world, and vision through a transparent lens and medium offers a simple common instance of consciousness quite immersed in its object. For the independent *being* of that world, action alone is the competent witness. For active concern with the object *must* find that object *self-guaranteeing* by its power; and that means existing independent of its being experienced. And that is why, in the degree in which we act rather than merely contemplate, we see the object for itself alone and our consciousness is identified with the object. To revert again to the eye for analogy: as the eye ceases to image the world at the blind spot where its message becomes effective by passing to the brain, so our experience ceases to be subjective when it becomes effective in action.

The position is like that of the American "New Realists" of 1915 and after; mind, in knowing, *is* the object. None of them, however, explicitly used the present thesis as an argument for independent or antecedent existence of the object. In fact it was one of them (Perry) who attained no little fame by coining the brilliant phrase "the egocentric predicament" (i.e., whatever you say or mean, about external reality, that reality is thereby related to you and no proof of existence apart from such relation is possible). And many have failed to see that the realists escaped this predicament any better than the epistemological idealist. According to our view, the criterion of action is the only available way out of it. And that is perhaps its novelty. In action, as contrasted with inactive contemplation, we are clearly delivered from the subjective trap, for we experience the object as being independent, self-existent at the moment. And this is true also of genuine contemplative knowledge, though contemplation has no means of proving it.

An objector might say: "You have chosen an extreme and desperate situation to prove your point. In ordinary life the concern with action is not so intense. Your example shows your own theory so desperate that it needs a desperate remedy." The answer is: it is matter of degree only. If one unconcernedly dons a hat or takes up a pencil to write, *just in so far* as he has active concern with the object is he aware of it as an external being existing for itself and by itself. And just in so far as at any time and place we find that we have to adapt our conduct to "stubborn" facts, so far we experience the stubbornness as something independent of our experience. From power alone can independence receive meaning.

We might put the objection in another way. When our experience merges with the object—as it does in contemplative thought —its separate identity is lost. But the same might be said of the object. *Its* identity is lost when object and knowledge become one. *Which* one? The epistemological idealist says, the experience; the extreme realist says, the object. So far there is a seesaw, as indeed the continued epistemological debates testify. The predicament remains: neither gets away from the factor of experience. But from the point of view of action, the object shows independence through power; and this power so occupies the experiencing mind that it becomes identified with that power. The balance, formerly even, now inclines to the side of the object. It alone occupies the stage, for it is self-guaranteeing by its power, while the experience-factor effaces itself by yielding to the stubborn fact.

Of course the mind does not always succeed in effacing itself in favor of the object: when it does not, there is error. But there is some true knowledge, and it is of that we are talking.

Note again the difference between this and the instrumentalist account. For the latter, chief emphasis is laid on action as a means of *controlling* reality. Man's own future experience is ever in view: he aims to order it more effectively, more intelligently. For our account chief emphasis is laid on action as a means of *adapting* man's life to superior powers (forces of nature, etc.). Consequently the instrumentalist finds the experience-factor essential and cannot admit a possible object quite apart from some experience; an experience, too, that is in some measure a determining factor in the constitution of the object. We, on the other hand, stressing the objective side, can easily see the subjective side becoming slender and transparent, self-effacing, and quite submerged in the object. Both accounts find the clue to reality in action; but our own does not emphasize the humanistic note, the control-aspect, and so is able to witness the category of independence.

Let us add to this but one more reflection: experience of the independent real may consist as much in sensing what *aids* our efforts as in sensing what resists them. Of this reflection no use will be made at present.

Our view is, after all, only the thoroughgoing application of the maxim that action takes a man out of himself. In the zero hour before we are called upon to preach, to race, to fight, the agony of self-consciousness is acute; as soon as we act, we regain the healthy-minded assurance and trust in the external world. We do not think of our own feelings, our own ideas, our own experience.

We are immersed in the objective state of affairs and the movement of events.

The result of our search for a criterion is this. Reality is primarily that power or those powers which we find we have to respect when we act to gain the ends we need. And of course this is not all. Real things have characters, qualities, relations, changes. These make up the content, the presentations whose reality we test by action. Our criterion is therefore twofold: it must use the test of presentation, and in its strongest form which is coherence; but this test is capped and crowned by the action-test which alone puts the keystone into the arch of presentations. And the corollary follows, that nothing can be accredited as real without a verification in our conduct.

But certain natural objections at once occur. To meet them will conclude the present account.

First: we are so loose in our terms! Have we precisely defined what we mean by *effort*, *feeling*, *resistance*, *object*, and above all, *existence* or *reality*? For instance: we say feeling of resistance amounts to feeling of a real object. By what right do we equate

these? We have first to know what we mean
by *real*, and what by *resistance*, and then to
discover that these meanings coincide. That,
we are told, is the proper, the analytic procedure. Analysis of meanings is prerequisite
to any understanding. Our argument is very
muddy. We might reply: the terms are clear
enough for the purpose in hand. The objector will counter: how do you know they are,
until you know all that they can mean? Some
meaning might crop up which would destroy
the whole argument. You can never proceed
with safety until you have precise elucidation
of each term employed.

But this objection misses the point. Precision is always a matter of degrees; and we
do not need a high degree of precision in our
terms. Some degree, of course, we must and
do have; enough to *denote*, but by no means
enough to supply full *connotation*. A man
may know that he feels a sharp pain without
knowing precisely where he feels it, still less
having a clear-cut definition of pain. So he
may have a feeling of muscular effort and of
a resistance located in some presented content, such as a heavy stone, without being
quite certain of the nature of muscle, or

strain, or stone. Not, of course, that he is *always* sure of even these feelings. Sometimes the effort is so slight as to be doubtfully present. Sometimes the power that resists is wrongly located: as when, for instance, with an arm "gone to sleep" the attempt to lift a pencil meets as much resistance as if the pencil were a heavy iron rod. True also, we may err in respect to what is the real object. What we are certain of, is the presence of *some* external reality. In the case of a paralyzed arm, the effort to move it is resisted by the physical properties of the nerves and muscles; *they* are the real external object, external to the desiring mind. But most times in normal life there is an unambiguous feeling of effort and resistance, with fairly correct location of the latter. It is the office of thought to locate correctly; of effort, to convey the existence-factor, the reality-coefficient.

Let us put our view thus: even from the perspective of thoughtful analysis, power, resistance, effort, and the like are primary elements in terms of which other things are to be defined. Definition comes down in the end to certain indefinables; these are the indefinables. Power and necessary connection cannot be defined in terms of mere presentation for the contemplative attitude. It was the keen analysis of Hume that brought this out, even while Hume believed, on practical grounds, in real necessary connection. The static cannot comprehend the dynamic. Rather must thought learn to take a category provided by another aspect of experience as its indefinable, ultimate term. Mind is polar; it is not (as the philosopher, always a thinker, is prone to believe) just thought. The conative and volitional aspect is deeper: it provides the foundation, while thought defines more and more clearly the superstructural details.

And here is an objection which against its will shows up the irreducible finality of the conative. It is suggested by the remark just made: we are not always certain that we *are* making an effort or that the presented datum *is* resisting. Didn't we then just assume that some efforts are real, not imaginary, and some resistances real, not imaginary? If so we begged the reality at once. By what right are real efforts distinguished from imagined ones? What is the difference between the thought of an act and the real act? We seem to need another criterion to support our own. And if none is at hand, we are back at the level of presentation; real acts will be those that hang together in a coherent order including the great body of our presented contents.

The objection is of the theoretical, contemplative type. It asks what presented character, describable for thought, distinguishes real from imagined action? In fact, there is none for thought. A real act is known to be real by being done, performed, entered upon; but these are tautological descriptions. Yet the doer knows immediately the difference. Thought can reach its threshold, but cannot cross it. Thought does not strive to *change* its object: action does. In this sense thought cannot comprehend action: action is thought's indefinable.

The proof of the difference lies in direct and immediate experience—the most immediate of all, since it is our very self that puts forth effort. Such effort cannot quite be reproduced in thought. Perhaps activity alone of all our experiences cannot be identically repeated in the merely contemplative attitude. The feeling of *effort when effort is being exerted*—where alone the contemplative experience of it is identical with the exertion—is not like other presented sensa, or qualities or images or other data of any sort. It is the extreme of directness and immediacy. True, the effort may be of different sorts: it may be muscular, or effort of intellectual attention, or of moral struggle, or desire of any sort whatsoever—for all desire is to some degree, and however misdirected, effort after what is desired. But the specific experience of effort is common to all these and in that experience is no separableness between contemplation and activity. The experience is perhaps as near to absolute simplicity—analogous to that of the divine being for scholasticism—as human experience can be.

The proverb says that hell is paved with good intentions. And rightly; a good intention is the thought of one's self as acting in a certain way, and contains usually also the glow of feeling that approves such action; but the single factor of effort put forth is lacking—that factor which in the end makes the difference between heaven and hell. The actual experience of effort, which can be gained only by voluntary exertion, can never be compassed by external contemplation—unless to some degree in the memory of past efforts made.

The point here brought out is perhaps the pivot of the whole position. The experience of effort is unique in a sense not found in other experiences. It contains an element of self-direction that is scarcely amenable to the usual categorial description by quality, quantity, etc. It eludes contemplation from outside the direct experience of it as the limit eludes the series, tantalizing, partially satisfying, never quite yielding.

Closely related to this uniqueness is the liberty of choice, always so incomprehensible to contemplative types of mind. In a sense it is true that no rational account of this self-direction can be given; it would have to be described as change, as caused, as quality felt, etc. But one who makes the experiment knows *that*, though not *how*, he can put forth effort in the choice of the moment.

But it is very hard for the professional thinker to admit this sort of thing. To him thought is the key to all reality: what can't be described and defined seems meaningless and he can't accredit the meaningless. So he will return to the attack: and probably as follows.

If directly felt effort were really different from the imagination of it, then it would no doubt give a clue to external reality. But there are cases where it certainly doesn't. Often in our dreams at night, we strive and struggle; but the men we fight with or the loads we carry uphill in those dreams aren't real. Therefore, effort is not the unique clue we have claimed.

The answer is that, at least normally, we do not really exert activity in our dreams. Rather we *think of* ourselves as doing so. We dream that we are running or climbing or otherwise performing, but we don't in the least energize our legs or arms. True, our legs may be tired from too long a tramp the day before, and this sense of fatigue may pervade the dream-consciousness. But then it is not muscular activity that we experience; it is the fatigue consequent thereon. Certainly in most dreams of our own activity something like this is the case. No doubt, however, in the fevered dreams of a restless night, when we toss uneasily in sleep, there is some actual exertion; for we do move our bodies then. And indeed then we *are* in contact with an external real, independent of our will. The real thing here is the physical muscle and physical brain, the latter with the diminished blood supply, and the inertia which inhibits the efferent nerve-current from brain center to relaxed muscle. And the latter *is* real indeed, and real independently of the desires of the dreaming mind. For the mind here runs up against the lethargy of the body which it cannot control. Do we say then that one's body is external to and independent of his mind? We answer, yes, probably always to some degree. What man is there that can make his body do exactly what he wants it to do? There is indeed a certain antagonism between mind and body—though doubtless partial and varying.

The like is true of more extreme cases. In a painful nightmare one *really* struggles with the *unreal* monster that sits on his chest—the discomfort or horror that one feels is a sign of the genuineness of the struggle. Well, we need here only ask: is there not really something there that we cannot get rid of? Usually that something is not at all located where in the dream we think it is located; viz., in the monster that sits on our chest. What precisely is it that resists our attempts to push off this monster?

The real object in this case is actually within our own body: not the hairy gorilla on our chest, but a load of undigested food in the stomach. It is a case of mistaken identity. And why not, when intellectual judgment is in abeyance? The practical criterion is responsible for the sense of reality, but not for the correct allocation and description. That is given by the coherence-test.

Further objections might be raised, pertaining to conflicts within the self. We make a resolution to drink no more cocktails, but the habit is too strong for us. Here it is the objective force of habit, a law which we certainly did not make, that is the independent real. Or we resolve to renounce the forbidden sweets of some immoral lure, and the struggle to keep on the straight path may be bitter indeed. Here we come upon the painful and too often tragic fact of the divided self—though the range goes all the way from the trivial choices between boiled and fried potatoes to the deep-lying oppositions felt in disorders of personality. The interests which are here in conflict are certainly independent of one another. So far are most of us from being the integrated personalities we should like to be.

Let this suffice for the account of the criterion of reality. Further objections might be mentioned, but the way of meeting them is perhaps well enough indicated in the above.

Now apply the criterion to the types idealism, materialism, and scholasticism. Are the principles they stand for, powers we have to respect in the conduct of our lives? Well, certainly we have to respect the minds of other people and the deeper needs of our own minds. So far the personalist thesis is well verified. What about the general systematic order of all things, that leads the monistic idealist to his all-including absolute mind? Do we have to pay heed to it in our lives? Up to a point, obviously yes. There is an order of nature, a system of laws, and we all do in practice believe in it. But we do *not* in our conduct pay respect to a *total* system. That sort of system is quite beyond verification. Remember that for the idealist it is a logical implication, an axiom of intelligibility. He accepts only the test of coherence. The absolute mind is not amenable to the practical test. So we must conclude that while order and system are real to a large extent, there is no satisfactory evidence that they cover the whole of reality. The monist is right in pointing to the presence of order, wrong in denying the possibility of some degree of independence, as in the personal minds. On the other hand, the pluralist is equally wrong in *denying* a one all-inclusive mind. It is all a matter of specific evidence, and that we have not got. And the like for materialism. The reality of the physical realm is constantly verified in our daily intercourse with the external world. But so is the reality of conscious minds. That is already given in our direct experience of active effort, which is the basis of the materialist's belief in physical things. The materialist is therefore wrong when he defines the very basis of his belief in terms of the objects he believes in; he saws off the branch on which he sits. He too, like the idealist, is right in what he affirms, wrong in what he denies. And scholasticism is in the same case. The general order with its given levels is on the whole well verified. What is not verified is the fixity and rigidity of this order. It *may* be slowly changing. Species *may* be evolving beyond their natural level. In fact, as we shall see in the next chapter, there is good evidence that they are doing so. Again, we find the type-view right in what it affirms, wrong in what it denies.

So the application of our criterion confirms what was suggested in the discussion of the types. The polar opposites of each pair—monist and pluralist, idealist and materialist, etc.—are to be taken as supplementing rather than denying each other. There is no evidence to show that one type has the ultimate truth and the others only relative truth. Ultimate truth, so far as we can reach it, seems to belong to all equally, though some systems (e.g., scholasticism) may provide a greater *number* of truths than others.

But of course this will not satisfy the idealist or materialist or other partisan.

Each one will declare that if he has got ultimate truth the others cannot have it. He
sees a logical contradiction in reality being
both mind and body, permanence and change,
one and many. One or the other of these
must be supreme; you cannot serve two
masters. And our pacifying eclecticism will
seem a weak compromise. Yes, there is here
a deeper problem which we must take up:
we must ask if there is really a logical
exclusion between the polar opposites. Later
we shall take up this problem.

Meanwhile we have got our first taste of
the all-welcoming attitude, and let us savor
its sweetness and fairness. And there is a
further taste to come. For, as we are now
to see, this all-welcoming attitude is the
very essence of the new type, the process-
philosophy, which we have not yet studied.
Remember our main thesis: it is the great
mission and message of this latest type to
show that nature herself contains a principle
of *growth by inclusion*, of combining more
and more opposites that once seemed uncombinable. This will be the topic of the
next chapter.

III

FUNDAMENTALS OF THE
PROCESS-PHILOSOPHY

IT is not easy to give a fair and just statement of our American process-philosophy as a whole. Perhaps it is impossible. Where shall we draw the line? Around Whitehead and Dewey, Hartshorne and Mead? Shouldn't James then be included? And even if we made some rather arbitrary selection, it would be no simple matter to discern all the implicit suggestions, the postulates inside that limit; for we are in the midst of the movement. It is the onlooker, not the player, who sees most of the game. Probably a future historian of philosophy will see the total setting of the movement better than we can.

But our aim is not primarily to attribute views with precision, or to give textbook instruction on a contemporary phenomenon —valuable as that is in itself. We seek rather to pick out and emphasize certain themes or notes of the present movement which seem to be of great significance for

the philosophic enterprise. Enough if these
notes are generally admitted to be there and
if their significance can be verified.

Two such notes we now single out:
(1) the new idea of process or change and
(2) the world as a continuum of experience.
Let us begin with the former.

The New Meaning of Process

The new meaning of process or change
can hardly be appreciated without some
account of its origin. It was slow in develop-
ing: the process-philosophy of today was not
born overnight. It has been taking shape
step by step for at least three centuries. We
might trace many factors in its history; we
might find it showing its infant head in the
gradual rise of the modern democracies, in
the new thought of human progress, in the
growing use of experiment in the sciences,
yes, in many of the conceptions of Spinoza,
Leibniz, Hegel, and so on. True enough, it
is rather exclusively modern. It shows no
explicit presence in medieval or Greek
thought. But modernity covers a period long
enough to develop a well-rounded and ma-

ture philosophy shared by many men with intense conviction.

For our purpose, it is enough to mark two of the high spots in this development. These two are outstanding because they show the two essential elements of the transformation of the common old notion of change into the modern notion of process. Change, for medieval and Greek philosophers, had been viewed more or less askance. It marked a lesser degree of being. If a man changed his views that meant they were not sound enough to hold their own. If a tree changed, withered, and died, that meant it was not strong enough to continue against the beating of wind and weather. What changed was weak, and weakness was lack of substantial being. Change was loss of being. The modern view, which sees in change a gain of being, had then to show two things. First it had to show that change is not wholly loss, but has a potency and power peculiar to itself; it is not negative but positive; a power of itself, a real and effective factor in the world. But second, it had to go further and show that change is not just one fact among others, but is the very essence of reality; for change to the process-philosopher is productive, increasing the sum total of being—in short, it is reality making itself.

The first step then was to bring change into the world of realities, and the second was to crown it king.

It was the work of Galileo that accomplished this first step. Galileo *experimented* upon bodies to see how they moved. He took them, put them in certain positions, and then watched and noted down, as clearly and precisely as possible, the motions that ensued. The experiments were but slight—practically nothing as compared with the elaborate experiments that were to come—but they were definite *acts* upon things which showed up traits of those things not noticeable to mere observation. And what was the outstanding trait that he discovered? This: the motion of a body, once begun, tends to go on and on in the same direction, provided nothing from outside interferes. With this law of inertia, later to become the first of laws in Newton's scheme, the modern notion of process was born. True, most thinkers have seen in the face of this tiny babe only the presage of a mechanistic quantitative science, of the uniformity of law common to heavenly and earthly bodies, etc. But there is more than that. Galileo disengaged the attribute *motion* from the then accepted system of the hierarchical order of nature. For the Aristotelian-scholastic view, bodies moved only so as to maintain their proper places in that order. The heavenly bodies moved always in the same paths; men and animals went about only to continue their being in the same environment; earth stayed below water and air above it, no matter how the winds blew and the torrents raged. Motion was subservient to order. And so indeed were other forms of change. They had no power of their own. But Galileo's result showed that motion of a body in a straight line, once begun, contained a tendency to go on forever. This tendency resided in the motion itself, and not in nature's effort to preserve a stable system. Motion, a potency for the older view, had an actuality, a positive character, *independent* of the hierarchic order. A stone, thrown with sufficient force, would fly out from the earth beyond moon, sun, and stars. There is something ultimately real in process. Not all reality is

Here

fixed terms (substances—accidents) and the relations between them. Process has a power and an ultimate reality all its own.

Let the point be emphasized: there was here a quite new idea. But the novelty was not the idea of process in the sense of flux; that had always been familiar and is still with us, an element in many a metaphysic besides the process-view. Long since, process had been attributed to Deity Himself; viz., in the emanation-theories of neo-Platonism. And the flux of nature was made ultimate by Heraclitus, and real by the Greek atomists, as well as by the Aristotelian physics. It is not process as change that is new; it is the power resident in process (so far only motion), the power of continuation *without respect to the general order*—that is the novelty. Hence we must say that *modern* process was then and there born.

But note that fixed order was not yet denied. No claim was made that the stars would be dislodged, or even a stone be thrown from earth with force enough to leave forever its natural home in the earth's soil. But a new power appeared, which, one might suspect, *could* work against the order.

The order is no longer the only principle. There is a principle of self-continuing motion. And it is this principle that in the future is to grow beyond all bounds.

Signs of this growth, indeed, at once appeared. The notion of process began to proceed. For instance: the idea of indefinitely continued motion in a straight line suggests the infinity of space; and we find the latter notion defended by thinkers who favored the new science. So Bruno and Descartes. And infinite space means a theater of endless possibilities; the notion of progress "onward and upward forever" is not too far distant, though not yet explicit. But it is not our concern to follow out this path. We have to do with a certain specific outgrowth of the general trend.

Come then to the second step. It was, once more, the contribution of an empirical natural science, this time the science of living things. In fact we see the two great divisions of science, the inorganic and the organic, physics and biology, contributing each its essential gift to the modern notion. The second contribution was of course the discovery of biological evolution. Living things were found to produce an ever-increasing wealth of forms. It is the note of increase, and (in a loose or quantitative sense) of progress, that marks this second step. To be sure, already before Darwin, something of the thesis of biological evolution had been suggested, as by Robinet and others. The nature of life, it was proclaimed, was to advance to new and higher, or at any rate to ever-differing forms; all life being derived from some simplest primitive kind or kinds below the level of the plant–animal distinction. A fixed order or scale of self-repeating species was ruled out. Indeed the notion of transformation was extended to the inorganic by Kant and Laplace. But these speculations only show the kind of ideas or hypotheses that were in the air. By themselves they could not give the weight of respectability that was needed, if the new notion of increase or progress was to be taken seriously. It was the work of Wallace and Darwin which verified the hypothesis of evolutionary progress. Not, of course, that the doctrine of biological evolution implied a necessary law of progress in the moral direction. But it did supply overwhelming evidence of a tendency to differentiation into ever new forms. It did paint the picture of the *growth* of the tree of life from a minute seed to an enormous trunk with countless branches. Though the biologist did not claim that this growth of the tree of life was necessarily a progress in the sense of increasing good, the *fact* of the dawn of higher and higher values, in the later reaches of evolution, was evident enough. Growth from lower to higher was thus to a considerable degree verified, and men could not but suspect a general principle of growth in living nature, not merely within the individual animal or plant, but of life as a whole. So wrote Bergson: "Nature is more and better than a plan in course of realization. A plan is a term assigned to labor: it closes the future whose form it indicates. Before the evolution of life, on the contrary, the portals of the future remain wide open. It is a creation that goes on forever in virtue of an initial movement. This movement constitutes the unity of the organized world—a prolific unity, of an infinite richness, superior to any that the intellect could dream of, for the intellect is only one of its aspects or products."[1]

Pause for a moment and witness here the transformation of the fixed hierarchy of the scholastic type. This is much the same notion as that, but in temporal form. The difference is that for the new view the higher grades come later. The medieval view pictured the grades of being as it were in a vertical scale from God down through the angels, man, the animals, plants, and inorganic nature to primary matter. The process-view was to picture emergent evolution so to speak in a horizontal direction from past to future, beginning with the lowest forms and ending with the highest. True, the highest stage for most of the moderns ends with man and his future progress; they tend to discard the supernatural. Yet S. Alexander was to write of the evolution of deity as the latest and highest step; and the modern personalist philosophy, with Whitehead and Hartshorne too, conceives deity as growing nearer and

1. Henri Bergson, *Creative Evolution* (New York, Henry Holt, 1911), pp. 104–105. Translated by A. Mitchell. By permission of Henry Holt and Company.

nearer to perfection. Allowing for differences in the particular stages, the general scheme is much the same, but for the change of direction from up-down to past-future. And no doubt the story of successive creation in Genesis is close enough to the picture drawn by evolutionism to support the transformation for many a devout Jew or Christian.

This analogy between the older and the newer view is instructive because it brings out the deep-lying and essential distinction of the latter; viz., its doctrine of process as increase in fullness of being: nature's principle of self-enlargement. We might put the case in terms of the causal relation. For the scholastic view, the cause is greater than the effect. Not only is it logically prior; it has a power which brings the effect into being, while the effect is so far not a power but a passive result. For the Galilean point of view, which is the mechanistic one, the cause is equal to the effect. The law of the conservation of momentum and of energy registers this equality. For the modern process-view, the effect is greater than the cause. Such is the doctrine of emergent evolution and of the incremental change which characterizes the growth of living things and of mind.

The main content and meaning of the new process-notion is now before us: it is not change alone, but change as a positive principle other than static order, and change in the sense of increase, or as it was sometimes called, creative change. No longer is change a loss of permanence or stable being, a mark of instability or inability to maintain one's being. That was what change meant to Heraclitus. That is what it still means to those who take permanence as a priori supreme requisite of the real. But this old view savors of the world of strife and opposition. It comes from the old world, so long a center of wars. For that old world, the strong man is he who maintains himself against all comers: the weak man is snuffed out, "bumped off," and the strong man does the "bumping." No, there is here an entirely different point of view. It is the view of peace and productiveness.

True being is not the sort of self-maintenance which destroys its opponent: destruction is in the end negation, diminution of being. True being is rather that which increases the range of being; fertility, production of the new, more and more without end. Surely there is more genuine being in one who produces much than in one who destroys much. And in this sense, too, did the scholastic conceive God the creator; and so far quite in line with the modern idea. But alas, in so doing he felt bound to rule out a natural increase of being in the creatures—which after all might have been a divine gift bestowed upon them. For to him, inheriting the Greek still contemplation of immutable, self-maintaining being, change meant instability; and if the order of nature is real, it must maintain itself on the whole unchanged. Yes, we have here a great root difference between the old and the new: the old world of war and the new world of coöperation and novel advance. There is no deeper difference known to the history of thought—no difference more significant in its bearing upon one's general attitude to life.

See then how the fundamental logical basis has shifted. On the one hand, being is and not-being is not. It is the logic of self-identity, with its three laws of identity, contradiction, excluded middle. It is the postu-

late of the scholastic, of the Leibnizian
monadology and to a degree, of its modern
form, personal idealism; yes, even of monist
idealism. For monist idealism, with its doctrine of internal relations, finds each real
thing in the world implicitly and finally one
with all the rest in the absolute mind. On the
other hand, the new view starts with a quite
different logic. Its postulate is not self-
identity: a thing is what it becomes, and
what it becomes is more than what it now is.
A thing is what it is to be. As Whitehead
writes, "The feelings are inseparable from
the end at which they aim; and this end is
the feeler."[2] And he adds, "If the subject-
predicate form of statement be taken to be
metaphysically ultimate, it is then impossible to express this doctrine of feelings."[3]
Transition, the *from-to* situation, gives the
essence of reality. As stressing this relational character, the from-to-ness, we are
evidently at the opposite pole to that where
all three of the preceding types are grouped.
They regarded reality as permanent being,

2. A. N. Whitehead, *Process and Reality* (New York,
Macmillan, 1929), p. 339. By permission of The Macmillan
Company, publishers.
    3. *Ibid.*

whether atom or mind, physical energy or
ideal values, or both; the new view regards
mere permanence of being as the fundamental
misconception of all past philosophy. Being
is not the term of thought, for term means
end, termination. Rather, being is the beginning or stimulation of both thought and
action; it is not term but relation. The new
philosophy tends toward, if it does not actually become, pure relationism. The first
great theme of metaphysics was *term;* the
second theme is *relation.* Yes, it is the greatest rift in all the history of philosophy. And
putting it in this way, we see the contrast
between the old oppositional attitude and
the new attitude of co-working productiveness. Terms are by nature exclusive; one
cannot *be* another. No meaning is any other
meaning. *Red* cannot mean *blue, wet* cannot
mean *heavy, I* cannot mean *you.* Terms dwell
in the region of exclusion and opposition.
No wonder that the spirit of conflict animated the older types of philosophy. But
relations are joiners. They connect terms,
referring one meaning to another for its own
fulfillment. Red is the complement of green:
how well they go together! Relation is the

adapter, the reconciler; it is the category that would overcome opposition, exclusion, and conflict.

Do we sense something of the lure of this noncombative and energizing outlook? Do we begin to feel that even if it is not yet strictly proved by fullest concrete verification, its hopeful confidence-giving suggestions should lead us to accept it as a working hypothesis for which we may well seek all possible evidence?

Well, so much for the first theme which we pick out as the significant contribution of our present-day process-philosophy.

The Experience-Continuum

Come now to the second element of process-philosophy. Here the treatment may be brief: the theory of experience is of relatively recent origin and has little of *positive* novelty, being rather a revolt against dualism than a constructive metaphysical hypothesis. It hardly dates further back than Mach and Avenarius in the later nineteenth century; it was taken over by James Ward and soon found a home with the Americans, James and Dewey, and others.

The teaching is that the events and things of the real world—minds, bodies, thought, motion, universals, individuals—are not ultimately irreducible entities as it were of different worlds, but are differentiations within the common matrix of experience. Whitehead writes, "The presumption that there is only one genus of actual entities constitutes an ideal of cosmological theory to which the philosophy of organism endeavors to conform."[4] And we all know his hostility to the bifurcation of nature into mind and body. So too Dewey: "The 'matter' of materialists and the 'spirit' of idealists is a creature similar to the constitution of the United States in the minds of unimaginative persons."[5] Matter and spirit differ in function and process, not in entitative stuff; they are but reified abstractions from the course of flowing experience. Nature is all of a piece; the word *experience* signifies this. Whitehead says: ". . . the energetic activity considered in physics is the emo-

4. Whitehead, *op. cit.*, p. 168.
5. Joseph Ratner, *John Dewey's Philosophy* (New York, Modern Library, 1939), p. 1053. By permission of Henry Holt and Company.

tional intensity entertained in life.''[6] But experience must not be understood only in the subjective way. It is not just your experience or my experience or the experience of some common or absolute mind. It is just as much objective as subjective. Nor is it a neutral entity or stuff, *neither* mental nor physical. Dewey writes: "Experience is *of* as well as *in* nature. It is not experience which is experienced, but nature—stones, plants, animals, diseases, health, temperature, electricity, and so on. Things interacting in certain ways *are* experience; they are what is experienced.''[7] Experience *becomes* mental in certain situations and in others it *becomes* physical. This view is here just as in respect of process, opposed to the earlier systems of idealism, materialism, and scholasticism, all of which declared that no body could become a mind, nor mind a body. Whereas idealism asserts that all is mind, and materialism that all is body, and scholasticism that mind and body are both ultimately real, the process-philosophy insists

6. A. N. Whitehead, *Modes of Thought* (New York, Macmillan, 1938), pp. 231–232. By permission of The Macmillan Company, publishers.

7. Ratner, *op. cit.*, p. 1041.

that mind and body are not only ultimately both real but are of one genus though with difference of phase or function.

For, after all, if mind and body are ultimately and eternally different entities, having no consanguinity of nature, it is impossible to see how they can interact or even be parallel to each other. The Cartesian dualism sets an insoluble problem. We must devise some hypothesis which views the mind–body problem in a new light; which permits them an obvious distinction yet finds within them a common nature that renders their interaction intelligible.

Thus the motive for the experience note in the modern view is not, like that of process, furnished by the discoveries of the empirical natural sciences. Rather it is furnished by a difficulty within the field of philosophy; viz., the mind–body problem. But notice its method of meeting this problem. Idealism, admitting the difference of mind and body, declares that both cannot be ultimately real, and (for reasons assigned) chooses mind alone as the ultimate real. Materialism, likewise admitting that both cannot be final reality, chooses (for reasons assigned) body alone as the ultimate real. These are both extreme views; they can contemplate no *via media*. But both scholasticism and the modern process-view do offer a *via media*.

For clearly the process-view is no extremist position. Whereas scholasticism finds the real things to be *either* mind or body, and in the case of animal and man both in one, this view too finds the original stuff of reality to be at least capable of becoming either mind or body. Both systems are synthetic positions which allow the real to be now the one, now the other; each adopts the *via media* that avoids the extremes of the other two types. But they take the middle way, as it were in opposite directions. Whereas scholasticism takes it by admitting *both* as fixed entities, process-metaphysic takes it by admitting *neither* as fixed entities. Scholasticism would avoid the mind–body problem, and in general the conflict between idealism and materialism, by granting that here the one, mind or spirit, is ultimately real, there the other, body, is ultimately real; and in man and the animals joined as form and matter. Process-philosophy would avoid it by de-

claring that one and the same reality is
potentially either.

But what is this reality that is potentially
either mind or body? Experience, they say.
And experience means the things, the sticks
and stones, storms, stars, the thoughts and
deeds of men, etc. Why then use the word
experience, instead of speaking of these
particular things?

With this question we end our account of
the second element, as enough for the present purpose. But the fact of the question
indicates that we must now pass to esti-
mation of validity.

And here, of course, we are bound to consider both the notes of the modern view.
Is the process-note verified as the criterion
of reality, given above, demands, and is the
experience-note in the same manner verified?

Critique of Process-View

Certainly *some* positive verification of the
thesis of process as incremental is at hand.
We constantly verify specific changes in
nature and in mind: in nature, at least living
nature, as evolution has revealed; and in
conscious minds the persistence of the past

in memory joined with the new experiences that are ever coming to us human beings, as Bergson has taught us. Perhaps this is not enough verification; we shall later consider that. For we shall take up first the question of the experience-motif.

When we consider the origin of this side of the process-philosophy, we find a decided contrast to the other, the new notion of increase. The latter was suggested by, and grounded on, specific empirical observation. Galileo and the evolutionists furnished the evidence. But the experience-theory was definitely not grounded on the discovery of specific facts in nature. It was grounded on the intolerableness of the mind–body problem, of the epistemological subject–object problem, and other like ultimate dualisms. The only claim for it is this, that no other hypothesis than that of a common experience renders these problems soluble; or rather, gets rid of them. In other words, the motivation and the grounds of the process-note are positive and at hand; the grounds and motives of the experience-philosophy are negative. There is a certain resemblance here to the Kantian deduction of categories.

The innateness of those forms of knowledge was for Kant the *only possible hypothesis* that would account for the synthetic a priori judgments made by physical science. But he could not directly verify the *innateness;* he could only point to the fact that we *do* think in terms of cause, substance, quantity, etc. The comparison with Kant's method is apt, just because it is so characteristic of process-philosophy elsewhere to prefer the method of verification to the method of implication, and to condemn the Kantian argument. For in this doctrine of experience their procedure seems to be: the hypothesis of experience is the only possible way of avoiding the rocks of dualism.

But after all, is this a fair account of their view? Is their "experience" just a hypothesis? Surely we must be very careful here: it may be that for them it is decidedly verifiable and no hypothesis at all.

Now "experience" is, as we might expect, conceived somewhat differently by different defenders of the modern view. We might here trace out an informing history of the notion, from Avenarius and Shadworth Hodgson up to Whitehead, Mead, and

Dewey. We might plausibly claim that with Avenarius it was more negative, more fully neutral, than with later thinkers, that it was next taken in a more subjective or psychical sense, as with Mach and James Ward, and subsequently in a more objective sense as by Holt when he wrote *The Concept of Consciousness*, and finally in a more inclusive, a less neutral and quite positive sense by the present defenders above named. Thus, for Whitehead it appears this positive sense is expressed as the feelings of actual occasions, each of which feels those feelings that have preceded it, where feeling "involves emotion, and purpose, and valuation, and causation."[8] Whitehead says: "Feelings . . . replace the 'neutral stuff' of certain realistic philosophers. An actual entity is a process, and is not describable in terms of the morphology of a 'stuff.'"[9] Yet this writer constantly assures us that consciousness is not necessarily present in such feelings, being rare and confined to high-grade occasions. It is of course very difficult to grasp the notion of feeling and especially of emotion

8. Whitehead, *Process and Reality*, p. 28.
9. *Idem*, p. 65.

and purpose without some tincture of consciousness. To many of us, feeling, emotion,
etc., *mean* consciousness. We cannot easily
find reason for using these terms unless some
consciousness is included. Apparently this
defender of experience finds no such difficulty, and it seems as if we could not meet
on common ground. Pratt has put the difficulty with his customary clarity: "Do I or
do I not *mean* by thinking and feeling and
willing anything which can qualify a physical
object in the way in which primary and perhaps secondary qualities qualify it?"[10] But
precisely here, perhaps, opponents fail to
sense the position of the reformer. For the
latter, feeling is a term including what is
common to *both* the material and the conscious, to wit, the fact (which all acknowledge) that each event, inorganic or living,
is *impressed* and *influenced* by preceding events
and reacts to the impression in its own way.
Now this impression is *analogous* to human
feeling, though the latter contains much
more. But that more is the original feeling-
element modified and qualified by the growth

10. *Philosophical Review*, March, 1936, p. 164. By permission of the editors.

of certain (conscious) attributes always latent in feelings. Thus, consciousness truly develops out of feeling: for instance, there is always in feeling an element of response (as in the animal noticeably) and a certain degree, however slight, of conflict between responses, a tension and tentativeness with the dawning future already making itself felt—and then we are at the portal of consciousness. Much the same view is taken by others, even others not of this fold, as in Montague's potential energy, energy held in suspense.

Thus what the neutralist does or means to do is to show how the attributes of consciousness are continuous with and latent in those attributes common to itself and to the physical; and doubtless we owe much to his analysis of the meaning of consciousness, especially in its active phases. It is certainly a valuable addition to the idealistic analysis of the intellectual phases, begun by Kant. Opponents, intent on defending dualism, overlook or belittle this positive service: a unique contribution possible only in the age of process. On the other hand, the neutralist certainly ought to show that those attributes *are* latent in the mere fact of feeling, as he defines it, and this he cannot do unless he is able to verify the presence of those latent attributes.

The point is that here he is just making an hypothesis, forced on him by the difficulties—theoretical mainly—of the mind–body situation. Now, by his own method, he is bound to entertain only an hypothesis which may be tested, which leads back as Dewey says to the material of primary experience.[11] But let us not underrate the grievousness of the dualistic *impasse*. It is a very powerful motive. It seems as if every other possible explanation of the mind–body relationship had been tried, and the experience-view were the only one left. Idealism and materialism each found it necessary to demolish body and mind respectively as ultimately real; scholastics alone bravely faced the problem, acknowledging each to be absolutely real, and attempted a rational account of their junction in man and the animals. They said: no form without matter, no matter without form (in the physical realm). The primary matter of man's body has no

11. Ratner, *op. cit.*, p. 1045.

being without its form, which is the rational soul, including all the powers incident to his conscious life. There is no puzzle, they said, as to how the two can be joined in one; the two can have no separate being, and their unity is a fact, not a problem. It would be a problem only for the Cartesian dualism, which sees in mind and body distinct substances: an artificial construct due to the Cartesian initial scepticism. The view is attractive and promising: it is significant that a nonscholastic thinker like Stout has come near to it in his thesis of the embodied self,[12] and another thinker, the idealist Hocking, finds mind to be the organization (form?) of the body.[13] No doubt in the inorganic elements matter and form are intimately related. The valency of a chemical element— a property due to its substantial form—is dependent for its "generation and existence upon a *determined quantity* of matter [atomic weight]. . . . Here the subjection of the form to its substrate is as profound as pos-

12. G. F. Stout, *Mind and Matter* (Cambridge, The University Press, 1931), Bk. IV, chap. 7.

13. William Ernest Hocking, *The Self: Its Body and Freedom* (New Haven, Yale University Press, 1928), chap. 2 particularly.

sible; the physical impossibility of breaking
it up without destroying it provides us with
an evident proof."[14] But when we ascend
from the corporeal forms to the intellectual,
found in man alone, we are told that intellect
has no special organ in man's body. Here the
continuity is suddenly snapped. Doubtless it
was a sense of this anomaly in the world,
this abrupt leap as it were into a new dimension, that inclined nonscholastic thinkers to
find the mind–body unity puzzling, and to
try one hypothesis after another to account
for the intimate relation between the two.
We need not here retrace the familiar suc-
cession—interaction at first with Descartes,
occasionalism, parallelism, panpsychism, and
their species. Even if dualism is right and we
are driven to the hypothesis of interaction as
Pratt so persuasively argues, it must still be
admitted that interaction has not been made
intelligible. Enough that the modern denial
of dualism is no more than a continued pointing out that since no solution seems attain-
able we must make the Aristotelian solution
thoroughgoing. Not only are mind and body
one in man; they are everywhere one in the
sense of being special forms or functions of

14. Mercier, *op. cit.*, I, 79.

the one all-present experience, the continuum of process. So argues the process-
metaphysic.

So, as we said above, experience is an
hypothesis and if it is not merely to remain
ad hoc it must be verified. Now surely it is
obvious that it has not been verified. In the
words of Dewey already quoted, "It is not
experience which is experienced, but nature—stones, plants, animals, diseases,
health, temperature, electricity and so on."[15]
And so, we might add, it is mental processes
and events too which are experienced. It is
specific things, events, qualities, even laws,
principles, or universals if you will. These
are verified and it is good scientific method
to accept them as real. Also it is permitted
to find collections of things or events real:
they too are verified as much as particular
things or events. It is even permitted to
speak of the whole continuum of things mental and bodily, if we take the word whole in
a loose sense and not as a closed entity. But
these are not what is here sought by him
who would solve the mind–body problem—
or deny its presence. He must show that the
two are not ultimately irreducible—which

15. Ratner, *op. cit.*, p. 1041.

means that they do have some specific traits in common, as in the case of Whitehead's "feelings." And he must verify the presence of those "feelings" as being in some degree of the same nature; they must be shown to be at least in part of the same sort when occurring in a mind as when occurring in an inorganic body. The common-sense dualist is persuaded that feeling as it occurs in a mind is absolutely irreducibly different in kind from feeling as it occurs in a nonliving body. Whether the monist has the greater burden of proof or not, certainly he ought to specify and verify as present both in minds and bodies some common elements.

Perhaps, however, we may get some clue to this common element, and some help toward specific verification, if we consult further statements by the process-school. We find Whitehead describing it as the "complex energy, emotional and purposeful, inherent in the subjective form of the final synthesis in which each occasion completes itself."[16] And elsewhere:

16. Whitehead, *Adventures of Ideas* (New York, Macmillan, 1933), p. 239. By permission of The Macmillan Company, publishers.

The primitive form of physical experience is emotional—blind emotion—received as felt elsewhere in another occasion and conformally appropriated as a subjective passion. In the language appropriate to the higher stages of experience, the primitive element is *sympathy*, that is, feeling the feeling *in* another and feeling conformally *with* another. . . . Thus the primitive experience is emotional feelings, felt in its relevance to a world beyond.[17]

And Whitehead *seems* to declare that this primitive experience ought to be verified. He writes:

But any doctrine which refuses to place human experience outside nature, *must find* in descriptions of human experience factors which also enter into the descriptions of less specialized natural occurrences. If there be no such factors, then the doctrine of human experience as a fact within nature is mere bluff, founded upon vague phrases whose sole merit is a comforting familiarity. We should either admit dualism, at least as a provisional doctrine, or we should *point out* the identical elements connecting human experience with physical science.[18]

True, we do not see the word *verify* in this statement; but the words (italicized above

17. Whitehead, *Process and Reality*, pp. 246–247.
18. Whitehead, *Adventures of Ideas*, p. 237. Italics mine.

by the quoter) *must find* and *point out* bear much the same meaning. Now it seems plain that such verification has not been given, by Whitehead or anyone else. Certainly no one has "pointed out" or can point out in a stick of wood the emotion with which it receives its impressions from light-rays, the warm sun, the breeze, etc. Even if we accept Whitehead's "feelings" as real, we do so from some general persuasiveness of the picture he draws of the world. Perhaps it is one of the most consistent and unifying, most coherent, of all the various pictures drawn by metaphysicians. Even so, we have learned that no such picture is to be accepted without specific identification of its main elements as met in practical life or experimental science. No, we must say that the experience-view of which we have been considering the most thoroughly worked-out form, has not been true to the code of the process-metaphysic, which is above all empirical. Once more we find suggestive the comparison between scholasticism and process; it will show how extremes meet. For as to the former both primary matter and substantial form are perceptually unverifiable—being inferences—so for the process-thinker are the solvent experience, the actual occasions and their emotions. The scholastic declares that observation gives only the properties or accidents of things, which are their specific acts and events and states; the modern view says much the same: "stones, plants, animals . . ." (quoted above) these things alone do we experience.

So the note of experience is not justified by good scientific method; it remains an hypothesis *ad hoc*, an escape from the realm of observed fact, where mind and body constantly interact, to a pure abstraction. For that is just what experience, proposed as a solvent of dualism, really is; its distinction from the particular objects and events makes it so pure and so abstract that it performs no explanatory service and has no verifiable effects. There is nothing more abstract than experience as such, as the matrix out of which mind and body differentiate themselves by difference of functioning. And as we might expect, a notion so abstract simply waits to be filled out and the different schools will fill it out in their own ways. To one, experience will connote some degree of con-

sciousness—so the monistic panpsychism of
C. Hartshorne. To another, it will be interpreted in a physical sense—so the naturalism
of R. W. Sellars. To others still, it will imply a dualistic panpsychism, as with Montague, Stout, Drake, Strong, *et al.*

And surely we may conclude that *any* attempt to view the inorganic world as of a
piece with the world of conscious mind in
the *qualitative* sense, is not open to verification. And there lies, perhaps, our great
difficulty with the monistic aspect of Whitehead's system. The feelings, the values, the
emotional intensity which he ascribes to the
nonconscious occasions of nature—these *may*
be there. But no *experimental* evidence shows
them. As we said in Chapter II, the real is
that to which in action we have to adapt
ourselves. Certainly we are under no practical compulsion to treat inorganic events as
values or feelings. No such test is made.
True, the large picture drawn by this most
genial thinker is so complex, so many-sided
and suggestive, that it provides a wealth of
hypotheses for metaphysical investigation—
and hypotheses are starters for all thinking.
And in its process-aspect, as will be seen,

there is a high degree of verification, perhaps more than we now realize. But so far
as one now can see, there seems no possible
way of identifying, in the fall of a stone or
the evaporation of water, any emotional
tone sufficiently like our own feelings of
value to bridge over the old bifurcation of
nature.[19]

We have not said the experience-theory
is false—only unverifiable, a mere possibility. We now make a further criticism and
affirm that in a certain respect it is verifiably
false.

We have seen in Chapter II that experience directly witnesses something beyond
experience. Hence we must reject out of
hand the experience-motif. We must not
only declare (what some of this fold might
admit) that the new functional definition of
consciousness and of body leaves them just
as irreducibly two as did the older sub-
stantive definition. We must go further and
declare that the world as a whole is, by all

19. The same point has been tellingly made in the essay by
Professor A. E. Murphy in *The Philosophy of Alfred North
Whitehead*, edited by P. A. Schilpp (1941), pp. 353–380, in
"Library of Living Philosophers," volumes published by North-
western University, Evanston and Chicago.

the evidence from our active life, *not* a continuum. There are breaks in it—many perhaps, but at least one break. External nature is not *always* or *necessarily* continuous with living organisms and their conscious behavior. Much of it is certainly quite independent of these: though perhaps in time it *may* become continuous with them.

For these reasons we drop the "continuum of experience." Continuum the world is not, in *their* sense; "experience" or "feeling" adds nothing to our knowledge.

Come now to the first note, that of process in the sense of increase—the note from which we name the new philosophy. We are about to see that we name it rightly; for it is the positive and serviceable element, largely verifiable and for the rest justifiable as a working hypothesis. And in the next chapter we shall find it both pointing to a settlement of the perennial quarrels and reaching forward to ever new perspectives.

If, as already noticed, common observation reveals much that is changing, the physical sciences seem to teach that everything is always moving. What electron or proton or neutron or radiant energy is ever

quite still, ever wholly potential energy?
And if moving, then changing, perhaps in
fundamental ways. It would seem then that
the permanent is a construction of the ab-
stracting intellect, and so on. Now here is,
up to a point, an obviously true position.
While it has never been verified that all
things are moving, still if it were possible to
estimate the amount of observed change and
of observed permanence in things, doubtless
the former would far outweigh the latter,
though some things do look permanent. But
the process-view goes beyond this. It makes
a universal claim for process. Yet it is quite
impossible to show by observation that there
are *no* permanent entities, no fixed unchanging nature, anywhere in the world. Empiricism does not suffice. There is then probably
another motive at work. And we do indeed
find one; the new view claims that if we do
admit fixed terms, unalterable structure, etc.,
we get into all the dialectical arguments and
disagreements that have characterized the
history of philosophy. If you don't admit
process everywhere, you have, say, atoms
indifferent to their successive and changing
groupings, you can't see why a proton

shouldn't behave to another proton as it does to a neutron. This dialectical appeal to the principle of internal relations is, however, of a rather a priori nature, not in the spirit of process; it sets up an ideal of what it means to understand anything. In the next chapter we shall see that there is no such ideal; but in any case it is not for the process-view, with its denial of rigid necessity, to postulate the rigid necessity that everything must alter with its surroundings. Dewey himself has said, "Variant philosophies may be looked at as different ways of supplying recipes for denying to the universe the character of contingency which it possesses so integrally . . . ."[20] Let not his own philosophy then deny the possibility of some permanent things or other.

No, we can find no warrant for exclusive process, process ubiquitous that forbids any unchanging atoms or electrons or even persons or God. Do not Whitehead's actual occasions become permanent and effective agents after they die? What is "objective immortality" but changeless reality? The occasions are real if they are effective—we

20. Ratner, *op. cit.*, p. 1048.

saw that in our last chapter. So impossible it is, in fact, to depict a world of *mere* process. And surely we should all have seen at once that the new notion of process, while it does make process everywhere present, includes also the note of conservation. The snowball would not grow unless it retained its core; mind could not increase without retention of the past in memory. Not only is there no evidence denying permanence; the very meaning of the new view includes it, though as *accompanied* by novelty.

The question remains, whether incremental process is *everywhere* present. Do minds at least tend always to grow, even if some of them seem to close up long before they die? Do living plants and animals tend always to vary more and more from parent to offspring? And is it possible that stones, stars, nebulae, even electrodynamic laws themselves, change in the direction of a richer variety of phenomena as time goes on?

Something of the third question shall be taken up in the next chapter. We shall urge that there is no logical necessity about the laws of nature, or the inorganic elements;

that there are no ultimate incompatibilities; that there may well be in nature, inorganic as well as living, a slow tendency to combine more and more of what seem to us now, or have seemed, to be incompatible conditions. Liquid air, fire that feeds on water, the fusing of electron and proton in the sun, offer suggestive instances. Particularly the notion of statistical laws inclines in the same direction; as if nature had an intrinsic tendency to vary in all possible ways in any given situation. We could point also to the "Mendelian" facts of heredity where the various possible combinations of genes seem to recur. There is, then, a body of decidedly specific evidence in favor of Whitehead's thesis of incremental process in the inorganic realm: and he might well have used more of this evidence than he did.

But of course for man the more directly significant questions are those respecting life and mind. Are these two essentially, intrinsically, progressive? We cannot doubt, of course, a fairly pervasive tendency toward increase, not only in the total volume of life, but also in its complexity, richness, and in the higher animals and man, felt values. But is this the whole story? Does it omit much that is peculiar to life?

As a fact, the great bulk of the species of lower organisms now extant have for ages changed relatively little. True, they have probably evolved somewhat; perhaps the bacteria we study today are somewhat more complex, somewhat higher in the scale of life, than those which lived a million years ago. But the degree of evolution we can verify in them is at most very slight. In fact, there is perhaps regression to some extent. So, too, with many other forms. How many of the colonial forms of plant and animal life have evolved into multicellular organisms? We do not know the number; but it is certain that many have not done so, since we find them today in the colonial form. Again, how many of the lower multicellular organisms of plant or animal life have evolved into the higher forms? Of course we do not know the proportion; but without question many have remained practically stationary in the long course of biological history, since we find at the present day a great number of these lower forms, such as lichens, hepatics, mosses, coelenterates, echinoderms, non-

segmented worms, molluscs, and so on.
The fact seems to be that relatively few out
of each lower phylum have given rise to a
higher phylum, relatively few out of that
higher phylum to a still higher phylum, and
so on. In short, as a significant phenomenon,
evolution as taken by the emergent-evolu-
tion view appears to be selective rather than
universal. There is no verified proof that the
amoebae, paramecia, etc., are showing signs
of any very significant evolution today. The
vast majority of species are and always were,
so far as observation goes, evolving so slowly
as to be almost stationary. On the other
hand, man does not appear to be so. We can
detect signs of progress in man: progress
not so much in bodily constitution as in
mental make-up. For without doubt there is
in man an accumulative memory, an increasing wealth of tradition and learning by experience; perhaps even an increasing moral
sense and reasoning power, which we do not
find in any of the lower forms. And presumably it is because thinkers like Bergson,
and other emergent-evolutionists are so pre-
occupied—unconsciously to themselves—

with man, that they find incremental process to be the deepest thing about life.

The fact seems to be that there are two broad tendencies in living things: the incremental tendency is one, and the other is the tendency to rest in what has been accomplished and repeat the same old life-cycle so long as it is successful. Even in man we observe the latter. Most individual men, having reached some more or less successful niche in the social milieu, tend to go on in the same rut, with a minimum of variation. Human societies vary more; their complexity gives a larger scope for the variation-tendency, and thus greater opportunity for growth. This has been impressively portrayed in Whitehead's *Adventures of Ideas*. But relatively few individuals, it seems, have a strong enough growth-principle to carry them much beyond the adopted niche. How few indeed get new ideas, new outlooks on life, after early middle age. (Particularly, alas! this has been true of us philosophers. It is almost true to say "once a materialist, always a materialist, once an idealist, always an idealist," etc.) With the lower organisms, the like is apparent enough, as has been already said. J. B. S. Haldane says, indeed, of the arthropods and vertebrates as a whole, that "degeneration is a far commoner phenomenon than progress."[21] Indeed, if this resting and repetitive tendency were not about as pervasive of life as the evolutionary tendency, how should we account for the persistence of the lower orders of life today? The bacteria, the algae, the protozoa, sponges, lichens, fungi, mosses, jellyfish, and so on—they are well adapted to the environment and there they stay. The Aristotelian entelechy applies to them in the main. Yes, some or many of their species did branch off in the remote past, giving rise to the higher phyla, classes, and so on; but the point is that also some remained. There is in life both a conservative and a radical trend. They are complementary; in a general way they coöperate to give stability in process; they differ much in degree, from the most progressive species, which have led to man, to the least progressive which have stayed at the level of the protophyta and protozoa.

21. J. B. S. Haldane, *The Causes of Evolution* (New York and London, Harper, 1932), pp. 152–153. By permission of Harper and Brothers, publishers.

In fact, the point is admitted by the process-view of Bergson, when he speaks of the torpor, the downward tendency, the nisus toward immobility found in plants, molluscs, etc. Whether or not he is right in attributing this nisus to the material aspect, matters little; since life has to have its material aspect. In any case it seems wrong to emphasize the progressive nature of the more radical species, and particularly of the upper reaches—consciousness and reason and intuition—to the *exclusion* of its polar opposite, the conservative factor.

Let us not say, then, that the new view *refutes* the older Aristotelian-scholastic view. Entelechy does seem to describe the stationary tendency fairly well, and that tendency is just about as ubiquitous as the progressive push of evolution. What the process-view has done is to increase our knowledge by pointing out a phenomenon, probably just as omnipresent as the entelechy, which had not been recognized by the older systems. And if process-philosophy does not claim to have refuted the latter, let us go with it wholeheartedly. Indeed, if it did so claim, it would not be true to its own spirit. Process, as already emphasized, is an inclusive notion. Increment would not be increase unless it retained the old in and with the new. So the higher animals, in a general way, possess much of the capacity of the lower, plus their own emergent qualities. Man has the growth-function, the sensibility and appetition of the lower animals, plus his own novel powers of reflection, reasoning, etc. The more willing should the modern view be to admit the repetitive tendency in the very constitution of the *élan vital*, providing it with the retained results of the past, the core of the growing snowball of life.

It is the note of process then in its inclusive and incremental aspect, which is to be welcomed as the valuable trait par excellence of this novel American type. The note of the experience-continuum is relatively valueless: it gives no novel element in the real world which can be verified, and is only an hypothesis *ad hoc*, conjured up as an escape from the troubles of the mind–body problem, etc. (Indeed in the next chapter we shall urge that such problems are not particularly troublesome.) But the emotional set, as well as the doctrine, of the process-note is constructive rather than destructive, productive rather than reductive. And this is what we hail as the new contribution, originating to be sure in the old world (in Bergson) but matured as a general principle of all reality— though not necessarily the *only* principle— in our young and forward-looking country of the extreme west. True enough, its leading thinkers, while they would if pressed probably agree with this inclusive attitude, have not in their works displayed too much of its spirit. They have all too often written to refute the other and older types of philosophy. Bergson reduces intellect from a truthful to a *merely* practical function, condemning alike the Aristotelian-scholastic entelechies and the mechanistic laws of nature to partiality and error; Dewey devotes many pages to demolishing the static and permanent as such. What we must here insist upon is that the positive principle of process does not rule out the truths which have been contributed by the older types that envisaged these other aspects of nature. Part of the burden of the next chapter is to show this specifically.

This, then, is the thoroughly democratic spirit of our native and modern contribution

to the thoughts of men, widening them with
the process of the suns. But though the spirit
be willing the flesh is weak. What we philosophers need to do is to purify *our* flesh—
that is, our intellects—so that we can *see
clearly* the compatibility of the other types
with one another and with the novel type,
and *show* the needlessness of their long-con-
tinued mutual refutation, thereby releasing
the strength wasted in barren controversy,
for discovery of more and more of the facts
and possibilities of the world about and the
world within us. At the end of the last chapter we viewed the various types as supplementing one another. And we took note of
the objection, which every type-view would
certainly make, that the opposites of each
couple contradict each other and, therefore,
cannot be peacefully joined. What is spiritual
cannot be body, what is permanent *cannot*
proceed, what is one *cannot* be as truly many
as one. The polar opposites are incompatible. To show their compatibility is then
our next task. We shall find, indeed, not
only that they are so, but that their compatibility is part of the compatibility of all
possibles, realizable without limit, which is
the heart and soul of the process-view.

A WORLD OF INCREASING POSSIBILITIES

Statement of Thesis

ABOUT the year 1885 a teacher in one of the best grammar schools of New England said to her class: "Every attempt of man to fly has failed. Time and again men have tried to make wings or other devices and perhaps sailed along a little way and then fell. The Greek fable of Icarus shows the truth. Man was not meant to fly." The statement is characteristic. Repeated failure so often leads to a universal judgment of impossibility. But a few years later the Wright brothers went ahead and made flying machines. Probably prehistoric man, before he had found out how to swim, looked at the fishes and ducks and said, "Ah! man was not meant to swim."

The point is that any judgment of this sort—so and so is forever impossible—is thrown under suspicion. After all, have we the right to say that any positive accomplishment is forever incompatible with the human make-up? Or even that the apparently

incompatible traits of nature cannot somehow be combined? As we view man's increasing power over nature we find that it
consists so largely in combining things
which nature herself seemed to show incompatible. Iron sinks in water, but an iron ship
floats. Wood and metals alike fall in air, but
the heavy plane flies. Organic tissue dies
when separated from its body but is pre-
served alive for an indefinite period in a
suitable culture. Sounds die out at a distance
but keep their strength unimpaired in tele-
phone and radio. The ultimate atoms are so
far beyond man's power of vision as to be
called mere concepts, but man invents the
electron-microscope. And when we think of
the well-nigh impossible feats accomplished
by our mechanical, chemical, and electrical
engineers, the suspicion deepens that ultimate incompatibles in nature are at most
few and far between.

Consider also man's nature as seeker of
ideal goods. All social progress consists in
combining the uncombinable. The intrinsic
self-seeking of the individual, his native disregard of others beyond his immediate circle, gives rise to warfare; warfare between

individuals, between closely tied groups, between nations. Man's problem is to make these hostile interests compatible with one another in a well-organized society. And however far he is, and perhaps always will be, from attaining his ideal, yet it *is* his ideal to find ways and means of joining interests that appear so utterly incompatible. And it is of course the moral ideal. Morality commands the abolition of incompatibles.

Turn now to another human value, the light counterpart of stern morality, the frivolous good of sport. Oddly enough, we find the same lesson. What is the essence of a sporting contest? You put forth all your strength to win the game; so does your opponent; you are beaten by a better man, you acknowledge it with equable spirit and thereby synthesize the inconsistent aims. In no other field is the discipline of the compossible so evident or so effective. The moral and social battle is won on the playing field.

These are social ideals; pass now to the individual. Here we find the ideal of a balanced character, *mens sana in corpore sano;* the combination in one person of interests in themselves conflicting. Your vocation is doctoring; your avocation is gardening or furniture-making; you would so adjust these that each, while served as a value in itself, also ministers to the other. To the child, all too many of his impulses are incompatible with one another and with parents' judgment; as he develops a character, adjustment gradually takes place. True, these examples are both vague and commonplace; but they point in the one direction; the ideal of maximum compatibility.

One more example: this one from the levels of man's knowledge, from simplest sense to abstract reason. There is in some degree a rising scale here, an increase of compatibility from lower to higher. Touch and pressure tell us of the presence of external bodies. But not many bodies can be touched at once and an animal having only this sense would, if thoughtful, deem it impossible to verify distant bodies. Hearing makes this verification possible; but with limited distances. An animal, given only these two senses, could hardly generalize to an indefinitely great distance. Vision alone informs the conscious animal of things at a practically unlimited distance, as in the case of the remotest seen stars. From the standpoint of touch, this distance-knowledge is incompatible with the very nature of verification; it is a miracle and a paradox. And when we add man's rational power a new paradox appears: we learn of things not sensible or verifiable even to vision: of tensors, $\sqrt{1 - c^2}$, laws and universals. Every higher stage is for the lower an impossibility; just as special relativity, now an accepted doctrine of physics, is contrary to the axioms about time-length which we used to take for self-evident.

Shall we not then say that the notion of incompatibles is the dead hand of the past, forbidding advance to new perspectives and more inclusive goods, of knowledge and practice alike?

But now listen to the other side. All very well, you say, in a general way, as regards man and to a degree external nature. Doubtless more things are possible than we used to think; more even than we now think. But do not be absurd. Man may cure more and more of his diseases, but he must die some time. He may break all the bounds set by the science of yesterday, but he cannot break nature's laws. Neither can nature break them. Wood cannot be a good conductor of electricity, a body cannot travel faster than light in a vacuum, a straight line cannot be the longest distance between A and B, no square can be round. We would make of imagination a spoiled child. We lose all principle. And here the philosopher joins in, with his special list of ultimate incompatibles; reality cannot in the last analysis be mind as the idealists say and body as the materialists say, or permanent as the Platonists urge and in process as the modernists declare, or intelligible as the rationalists say and above all comprehension as the mystics allege. Yes, even the unbelievers, the philosophical sceptics, say the same. They point to the age-long opposition of philosophic systems, as bitter today as ever, and see in it a proof that man was not meant to philosophize. No, it is not merely the old fogy who posits limits to human attainment. The highly cultivated sceptic, equipped with the most refined up-to-date analysis, puts more limits than the old-fashioned metaphysician.

Yes, probably most people will agree that there are ultimate impossibles, insoluble in-

compatibles—even though they differ as to
what these are. And let common sense keep
this belief; for it seeks the directly practi-
cable in our given environment. But philosophy would probe deeper; it would ask if that
environment shows signs of adaptability to
ideals hitherto deemed unrealizable, signs
of growth toward a state where the incompatibles of the past are reconciled—where
the lion shall lie down with the lamb—and
where the future opens ever wider and wider
in its possibilities, and without limit.

To answer this question affirmatively is
our thesis. We take heart at man's liberation
from one dogmatic limitation after another,
and declare that there are no eternal a priori
restrictions on reality, no universal criteria
pinning it down to some one form rather
than another. It may be this, that, or the
other, or all together. There are no ultimate
incompatibles. It may in the last reckoning
be mind and body at once, at once permanent
and flowing, one and many. And so the time-
honored hostilities of the schools have no
ground; idealism and materialism, scholasticism and process, monism and pluralism may
all be true together; the stigma of unpro-

ductiveness due to perennial disagreement is removed from metaphysics, releasing its energies for the discovery of ever new perspectives, ever new ways of reconciling the irreconcilables, of envisaging new permutations and combinations of the elements of reality.

The present essay will treat only the negative aspect; it will array the evidence for the denial of incompatibles. We must remove the stumbling-block before we can advance. The positive aspect of the thesis reveals compatibility as a living force in the actual world, namely this: there is a tendency, verifiable throughout nature, to realize all combinations and permutations of things and events—a process without limit, the growth-principle of nature, or principle of plenitude as Lovejoy called it. The evidence for this belongs to another occasion.

Of course, as a plain fact, the world about us is pretty well ordered. It has its laws, of electric attraction and repulsion, of radiant energy, etc.; and we do believe that they are not very much broken. There are plenty of thinkable events incompatible with those laws. A mermaid couldn't live in any of our waters; a path along the Equator from Brazil to Africa couldn't be the longest distance. But our thesis is that there is nothing intrinsically necessary about the present order. It is but one among many possible orders. And there is no reason to deny that it will change: perhaps is even now slowly changing. Whitehead has already suggested this; but we go further than he, and assert that there are no absolute or ultimate necessities at all, not even in the realm of eternal ideas. There is no such thing as intrinsic logical implication between any one entity or meaning and any other: be that entity an event, process, thing, term, proposition or what not.[1] All logical implication is extrinsic: read in at the beginning by postulation or arbitrary fiat, and then read out again as a deduction. So the compulsions we find in the laws of our order are the compulsions not of reason but of power, like a gravitational pull or the force of a man's desire. It is not what rationalists have argued for as an a priori demand of intelligibility. This ideal of in-

1. As Aquinas says: "But if we take away the impossible, then we destroy also the necessary." *Summa Theologica*, I, Q. 25, Art. 3, Objection 4.

telligibility is not an ideal but an idol, derived from the false belief in the intrinsic deductive necessity of reasoning. But all reasoning is tautology. It is like the game of chess. The rules of the game are the postulates; they state at the beginning how each piece can move from every single square. They are summary statements *already understood* to include every possible move and every possible combination of moves. Their so-called implications are deliberately planted in them at the outset. If we are told that a pawn may move forward one or two squares, and proceed to move it so, we have scarcely unearthed any novelty not contemplated in the rule. And the like if we add a knight or a bishop or all the rest. But the players, being human, cannot intuit all these possibles at once; they discover them gradually as they play. So it seems to them that the postulates or rules of the game generate new situations not present at the beginning. Such generation is a fiction.

There is implication only where implication has been created by fiat or power or whatever you may call it. Deductive inference is not logical but psychological. There

are no ultimate necessities valid of themselves; no ultimate incompatibles. All things
are compossible. Is it necessary to add that
the phrase "all things" refers to positive
qualities, entities, relations, events, terms,
propositions? A proposition and its denial
are not two things in this sense; of course no
proposition is compatible with its denial.
We are not going to reject the law of
contradiction.

Something like this is our claim. And if
the statement of it does not appear to lessen
its flavor of perversity, let us remind ourselves of the metaphysical significance and
promise that it bears.

The Evidence

Our method will be to take one outstanding case after another of alleged necessities
or incompatibles and by analysis of each
round to the general conclusion.

Take first the most stubborn, supposedly:
the realm of mathematical truth. A typical
outstanding case is that of the round square:
the same figure cannot be both round and
square. But consider an observer looking
down on a semicircle from a point above it

in the same vertical plane and the semicircle concave to the observer. To him the curve will appear as a straight line. Now place an equal semicircle in a vertical plane at right angles to the first, so that it is convex to the observer, and the two semicircles are joined at one end. Each of the semicircles will appear a straight line to the observer, and the two lines will form a right angle from his point of view, while from a point below and outside either plane they will form a wave-figure ∽. If this situation is repeated to give four such semicircles in a closed curve, the observer from above will see a square and an observer from the side will see nothing but roundness. The same figure is square or round according to the observer's situation. Seen as a two-dimensional figure from above it is a square with no roundness. Seen as a three-dimensional figure from the side it is round with no squareness. But if we regard the figure as in both two-dimensional and three-dimensional space at the same time and place, then it is both round and square. We need only postulate for the second dimension the properties of the third in addition to its own. True, in our given natural order, these are not combined; nor can our given senses intuit them so. But their combination is conceivable and definable. When, then, we declare round and square incompatible, we should add—incompatible with our actual Euclidean or near-Euclidean world. But there is no known a priori necessity about this actual space.

The example is like others. In Flatland you can't go from one side of an endless line to the other without crossing it; add the third dimension and you can. Nor can you go from one side of a finite plane to the other without going over the edge; but twist a ribbon through 180° and join the ends, and you can. Again, the meridians of longitude are parallel at the equator and yet without changing direction meet at the poles. Many properties incompatible in a lower are compatible in a higher dimension. And why? Because in a higher dimension the restrictions are removed. And why should they not be? The only answer is that in our given world they don't seem to be. Again no intrinsic necessity or incompatibility has appeared.

But, you say, a round square is certainly incompatible with a space limited to two dimensions. And this is true, but tautologous. Plane geometry (typically) *means* by straight the exclusion of curvature; it *postulates* at the beginning that a figure made of straight lines cannot be curved. There is no inference: just a definition (postulates are the definitions of indefinables). Do you insist that the definition is not arbitrary but forced on us by the nature of our space as we observe it? Yes indeed, we agree. But our space is just the given order of things and no definite reason why it must be has been assigned.

Take now an instance from the field of number. Is it not impossible for a negative number to have a square root? Now common sense represents numbers by unit lengths along a straight line in either direction from a central point 0: a one-dimensional scheme. Negation here means reversal of direction along the line; the negative of a negative number is a positive number, and -1 negated becomes $+1$. This is the way in which common sense defines negation and negative numbers; it postulates, on the basis of observing a line, that the negative direction is the reversal of a positive direction, but not of a negative direction. Which is to say that *in one dimension* a negative number is not the product of two negatives or of two positives; i.e., not a square number. But there is no possible inference to the general conclusion that in *more* than one dimension a negative number cannot be a square number. Take the case of two points A and B, end-points of the diameter of a circle, and let them be, say, one inch apart on the circumference. Then $2AB = 2 = AB - AB = 0$. If you go around the circle you are back where you started. The rule of straight-line number does not apply. But more: $AB = -AB$. One inch in either of the opposite directions from A lands you in B. Plus one taken once in the positive or right-hand direction lands you at B which is minus one inch from A. So the square of plus one is minus one and conversely the square root of minus one is plus one. Of course all this holds only because number is now interpreted in a two-dimensional scheme. But it may suffice to show that $\sqrt{-1}$ contains no internal incompatibility except the terms plus and minus be *already defined* in *mutual exclusion* or what is the same thing, incompatibility—as they are in linear dimension. In general it would seem that a higher dimension is but a way of seeing that supposed incompatibles are not really such.

But now an objection. Surely, there must be some limit to the number of dimensions. Suppose, then, there are some day discovered to be just 365 possible dimensions. Then the properties so far found incompatible are ultimately incompatible. There is no higher dimension to render them compatible. In fact, why not at once leave the realm of petty instances and mount sky-high to an all-visioning statement: every thing or event, to be at all identifiable, must have its identifying traits, its nature distinguishing it from others, ruling out the traits of those others. A cat cannot wag its tail for pleasure as a dog does—it would not be a cat. It is incompatible with felinity. An angel cannot walk and be tired like a man: it is incompatible with angelhood. And so on. If there is to be any identifiable reality at all, there must be definite things with definite natures. It is incompatible with individuality to take on too much compatibility. Have we not here an implication, absolutely a priori, valid in any kind of a world, drawn out of the very meaning of reality itself?

Now, it is one thing to argue that there must be incompatibles and another to point out some specific ones and verify their internal inconsistency. The above objection will remain unsatisfactory so long as it fails to point out specific cases. It is a fact so general as to look like mere tautology. We are informed that each thing must be itself, true to its own nature. This is the old law of identity. Does it rule out change? Surely not of every sort. A cat may move from here to there, may wave its tail too, but not in joy. True, of course; but may not *Felis domestica* evolve in the ages into an animal that does wave its tail in joy? True again, it will be no longer the same species: but the new species shows the compatibility of the two traits. In fact, the course of biological evolution as a whole seems to show in the higher species a compatibility of traits that were incompatible in the lower species. We have already noticed this in respect of the evolution in man of higher senses from lower and of reasoning from sense. But the argument might be carried on indefinitely. The amoeba could not remain an amoeba and move about as the coelenterate jellyfish can do. The coelenterate could not form societies as do the insects without the rich instinctive responses that are found in the latter. The point is obvious and needs no detailing. Surely it is not amiss to describe evolution as the appearance of new orders of life, new species, such that on the whole the later orders show a gradual increase of compatibilities. Grant, if you like, that there must always be some sort of order in nature; there is no arguing from that to the permanence or necessity of any one specific order. Our thesis was stated to be that every order permits change to any other.

It does not deny causal laws. But if in any given order, a specific cause A is followed by a specific effect B, we do claim there is no intrinsic necessity for B. In another order it would have been C, or D, etc. Mere causality, causality in general, permits any kind of detail you please. It is compatible with *any* particular laws; even, as we shall later see, with chance variation. No, the above objection, weighty as it at first appears, is too abstractly universal to have specific consequences.

But, in fact, the objection has been treated too respectfully; for as was just said it states no more than a tautology. It is talking of finite individuals distinguished from one another and to be sure they must be distinguishable if they exist. But who has shown that reality *must* a priori comprise such beings? Why not God alone, a single being, in whom are contained, in perfect compatibility, all possibles and compossibles? We shall in the sequel come to this: but for the present no evidence has appeared which would rule it out.

And now let us parachute back to the ground of particular instances.

A is greater than B, B is greater than C, therefore A is greater than C.

At first this looks as if the relation between A and C were something quite new, not already contained in the relation between A and B and the relation between B and C. The reason why it looks new is that in general we cannot tell what the relation between the first and third term will be. *Greater than* happens to be a transitive relation; but many relations are intransitive. Why is *greater than* a transitive relation? Because that is the meaning of quantity: it is one of the postulates used in defining quantity. We do not first have the notion of quantity and then generate the notion of transitivity out of it. It is quite possible to conceive specific kinds of *greater than* in which the relation is intransitive. A is west of B and B is west of C, but if these lie on the earth's surface, A will also be east of C, or even at C itself. If any one argues that there is something in the very nature of quantity that compels *greater than* to be transitive, it is up to him to point out what that something specifically is. Those who defend logical compulsion do not do this. They just assert that such and such an attribute follows from the *nature* of the thing. Clearly, this is just the "dormitive power" of opium over again.

Perhaps you say the transitiveness of *greater than* is necessitated by the other postulates that go to make up the definition of quantity. But this cannot be so. For the criterion of a sound system of postulates is that they are independent of one another. Perhaps the signal contribution of the modern habit of postulates is just this: it lays the ghost of logical necessity between the elements of a system. Systems are not inevitable; they are fiats, whether laws of nature made by a first cause, or schemes of possibles made by man.

But quantitative reasoning might be admitted too specialized to offer strict a priori necessity. So now the rationalist brings up a case which does seem to possess it: a case so general as to seem unconditionally true. A implies B and B implies C, therefore A implies C. Surely there is more in the conclusion than in the premises; viz., the relation between A and C which the premises don't mention. And no one would think of denying the conclusion. Here, if anywhere, is ultimate logical compulsion; perhaps the primeval case.

Now for argument's sake let us assume that implication is a meaningful term. We shall see in a moment that even if it is, this is not an instance of it.

When we know that A implies B and B implies C we have in thought traced out a journey from A through B to C. Whether we *had* to take each of the two steps is really irrelevant. The logic of the journey is quite the same if for *implies* we substitute *happened to be followed by*. A man may move, let us suppose of his own free will, from a point

A to another point B and again of his own free will from B to another point C. Then the inference holds, just as necessarily as if the movement were compulsory, that to go from A to B and from B to C is to go from A to C. The strength of the inference does not in the least depend on the meaningfulness of implication between A and B, and between B and C. It is just the relation of passage, not of necessary passage, that is pertinent. In short, the notion of implication plays no part in furnishing the synthetic inference from A to C.

The journey from A through B to C is before us, laid down in the premises. We have gone from A to B and from B to C. Could anything be more obvious than this: that the conclusion, instead of extending our knowledge, drops out part of it? It tells us that we started from A and arrived at C. We knew that, of course, as soon as we had our premises. The only difference is that we neglect the intermediate point B. It is not a case of rounding to the whole from the parts, not a synthesis of two elements to produce a new element. We had arrived at C by the end of the second premise. We had the

whole before us by that time. In the conclusion, instead of conjuring into being some
new entity, we simply thin out our survey of
the whole, to a line joining the end-terms.
What man of common sense, having gone
from Boston to New York one day and from
New York to Washington the next day,
would see novelty in the statement that he
had gone from Boston to Washington?

A mountain climber plods up the steep
path now walking, now pulling himself up
over rock, intent only on the details, and
when he reaches the top and the view of the
long and hazardous path he has ascended
bursts on his amazed vision, he finds the
synthesis a true novelty. But he confuses the
novelty of the view with the tautology that
the whole of his climb was the sum of the
steps. So the reasoner who solves a long and
intricate problem, forgetting the parts he
has gradually summed together, feels the
novel triumph of this particular victory, the
reward of his toil. Let us say then that the
notion of implication is drawn from the emotions of surprise and gratification after a
successful labor: emotions which the clever
man who sees through the problem at once

quite misses. Inference is a psychological not a logical category.

And the like is seen in that other apparently unconditioned and a priori necessary instance, the syllogism. Logically speaking, the syllogism is surely a tautology: we couldn't be *certain* that *all* men are mortal unless we already knew that the *particular* man we are going to infer to, is mortal.

But, as Montague has pointed out,[2] we do not first *prove* by this well-nigh infinite enumeration that each man is mortal. We just have a sort of general confidence in the mortality of human beings; we have not explicitly included each particular case in this general confidence; and to this extent the syllogism is not a tautology. *To this extent*, however, means *as a psychological affair*. To the individual thinker, as a conscious person thinking along in time, the thought of Socrates is not before his attention as soon as he thinks "all men are mortal." The minor premise and the conclusion unfold the properties of the total assertion about all men; they were already tacitly lodged in the very

2. Wm. Pepperell Montague, *The Ways of Things* (New York, Prentice-Hall, 1940), pp. 31 ff.

meaning of the term "all men" but they had not come to clear, conscious recognition. The syllogism performs the service of bringing these so-called consequences to explicit presence in the mind. It is, indeed, a great service, and here lies the value of formal logic: it reminds us of what we really meant but had hardly realized. It is like recalling to a man a promise he made which he has forgotten, but for which he is morally responsible and to which he is committed.

The wholly psychological nature of the novelty in the conclusion is even more evident in the well-known story of the priest who told some ladies that his first penitent was a murderer. A moment later entered a nobleman, their much-admired neighbor, who remarked casually that he was the priest's first penitent. The horrified surprise of the ladies only shows that they did not know the ground of the abbé's statement; they took it on authority from him. But *he* knew its ground, and for him the syllogism was pure tautology—as it was, too, for the marquis.

But have we yet given the case fair trial? We have taken rather isolated statements, small bits of reasoning, so small that they can easily be made to look like tautologies. We ought rather to examine longer trains of reasoning, where the last propositions do at least look to be very different from the first.

Agreed. Let us then take up such trains. The first is drawn from a modern work on the foundations of mathematics,[3] and the second is a simple algebraic problem about moving bodies. The first is more abstract and general, the second brings us nearer to the actual world.

"Let us choose a few simple propositions from euclidean *plane* geometry, and see what we can derive from them formally.

"1. If A and B are points, there exists a line containing A and B, . . . we are certainly obliged to leave 'point' and 'line' undefined" (pp. 38–39). The writer adds some further assumptions about points and lines, which are not relevant to our purpose. Now, before we go further, note the statement about leaving "point" and "line" undefined. It is

3. John Wesley Young, *Lectures on Fundamental Concepts of Algebra and Geometry* (New York, Macmillan, 1911). By permission of The Macmillan Company, publishers.

somewhat misleading. Points *are* defined as components of or contained in a line, as having lines passing through them, etc. Lines also are defined by their relations with points. In general, the postulates of a given set are the definition of the so-called indefinables of that set. Professor Young indeed admits it later: "As far as their logical character is concerned, *the unproved propositions* [postulates] *play the rôle of disguised definitions*" (p. 53). So remember that we do not really start with infertile indefinables which become fertilized by the action of postulates. We truly have the whole thing given at the outset: postulates and terms are one.

Let us now proceed to the deduction of theorems. We start with seven postulates. The first two tell us that any two points determine one and only one line:

"1. If A and B are elements of S, there exists an m-class containing A and B.

"2. If A and B are distinct elements of S, there exists not more than one m-class containing A and B" (p. 41).

Postulate 5 tells us that every line contains also a third point at least and Postulate 7 assumes that there is such an actual entity as a line:

"5. Every m-class contains at least three elements of S.

"7. There exists at least one m-class" (p. 41).

So far then the postulates tell us that there is before us one line containing three points, and that if there are other points outside the line any pair of them uniquely determines a line. Postulate 6 now tells us that there are points—one at least—outside the line already given:

"6. Not all the elements of S belong to the same m-class" (p. 41).

What we now have, then, is a line containing three points, and another point outside the line, and the assurance that each pair of points contained in the assemblage of four determines uniquely a line, and also that every line contains more than two points. (Postulates 3 and 4 may be here omitted as they concern parallels and are not used in the first paragraph of Professor Young's deduction, which is all we deal with.) The deduction proceeds to show that whereas we started with three points on a line, we prove by the postulates that there are at least seven points (p. 42): as if there were a real productiveness. Now consider what the postulates have told us: (1) *Given* is a line containing three points (1, 2, 3 as Young calls them) (Postulates 5 and 7) with another point 4 outside the line (Postulate 6) and two lines connecting 4 with 1 and 2 (Postulates 1 and 2), which lines contain respectively a third point 5 and 6 (Postulate 5), and also a third line connecting 1 and 6 (Postulates 1 and 2) which contains a point in addition to 1 and 6; viz., 7. This is what the postulates tell us. We have made no new statement over and above the postulates, *except to name* the several points and to *regard* each point and line as fulfilling the postulates. The procedure for each separate inference is just this: the postulate is true, this line or point is an instance of the postulate, therefore this line has the property announced in the postulate. It is a syllogism in Barbara. That, indeed, we have already examined, and found tautologous. So then is this mathematical reasoning.

As we said at the beginning, it is like a game of chess. The moves of the pieces are stated in the rules. Every move is an example of those rules. Every combination of moves, every game, is likewise an example of them.

We give one more example, this time from the nongeometrical realm of linear order which is the basis of number. Let us begin with a relation symbolized by < "which we assume as *undefined*" (p. 68). (Of course, in accordance with the quotation from page 53 above given, the postulates are going to define <.) But meanwhile the candid author remarks, "This symbol may be read 'precedes,' 'less than,' 'above,' 'older than,' etc.; but care must be had in using these words not to attribute to the symbol any of their possible connotations which are not implied by the assumptions presently to be made regarding this symbol" (p. 68).

"The expression a = b (read: a 'equals' or 'is the same as' b) [note particularly this last phrase 'is the same as'] indicates that the elements a, b in question *may be interchanged* in the discussion [italics mine]. The expression a ╪ b (read: a 'is distinct' or 'is different from' b) indicates that a and b may not be interchanged. The relation $<$ is then characterized by the following *fundamental assumptions:*

"Given a class C and a relation $<$; let a, b, c be any elements of C.

"If a $\neq$ b, then either a $<$ b or b $<$ a.

"If a $<$ b, then a $\neq$ b.

"If a $<$ b and b $<$ c, then a $<$ c.

"It follows as a theorem that if a, b are any two elements of C, we have either a $=$ b, or a $<$ b, or b $<$ a" (p. 68).

The tautology between this theorem and the assumptions is obvious.

Come now to the second and more concrete of the two examples above promised; viz., the simple algebraic problem about moving bodies. John rows five miles downstream in an hour; he covers the same distance back upstream in two-and-one-half hours. If his rowing is at a constant rate and the current likewise, what is the velocity of the current? Most people would say that the solution is a matter of deductive reasoning, a synthetic judgment from a premise A to a quite different proposition B as the result. But see how we reach the solution. Denoting the required rate of the current by x, we

write down the equations x + John's rate =
5 and $- x$ + John's rate = $2\frac{1}{2}$. Subtract the
second equation from the first: $2x = 2\frac{1}{2}$ ∴.
$x = 1\frac{1}{4}$, the rate of the current. John's rate
is then $5 - 1\frac{1}{4} = 3\frac{3}{4}$. Note that the
premises yield the conclusion by means of
equations, and that the equations are statements of identity between quantities. The
first two equations are mere symbolic statements of the premises. The subtraction of
the second from the first is an instance of the
definition of subtraction which is one of the
postulates of number. The like is true of the
final division of $2\frac{1}{2}$ by 2 to get the value of
x. The problem is of the same nature as this
one: if $2 + 2 = 4$, what is $4 - 2$? The propositions are always equations; they deal in
terms of postulated identities. Something is
numerically or quantitatively identical with
something else, and certain parts of each are
identical, whence the remaining parts, which
are the ones we are interested in, are identical. That is the way we reason: it is but an
instance of the postulate that if equals be
added to equals, the results are equal—and
so on. It is just as if we posed the following
situation: "One man is pushing another and
weaker man against the wall. What is hap-

pening to the other man? Answer: He is being pushed against the wall." The only difference is that the strength of the pushes is stated in our example—the strength of the rower and of the current—and the event instead of being almost instantaneous, takes three-and-one-half hours. Ordinary intelligence answers that the weaker man is pushed against the wall. The answer to the above problem is of quite the same sort, granted the postulates of the numerical operations, addition, subtraction, and division. The only reason why there *seems* to be implication and increase of knowledge from premises to conclusion is that the ordinary mind is not clear and quick enough to see the conclusion the very minute the premises are stated. In fact, the mathematical genius is the man who does at once see the conclusion, just as Mozart is said to have heard his whole symphony at once while he was composing it. Seen in this light, implication is only another word for lack of vision—of *immediate* vision. In brief, consciousness of implication is in direct proportion to stupidity: the obverse of stupidity; deduction, as said above, is a psychological not a logical advance.

But we have lingered too long among ab-

stract concepts and propositions and problems. In such a realm, no doubt, one is at
liberty to imagine or postulate more or less
as he pleases. But the real world is what
can't be imagined away. Concrete things
compel the mind. Probably then the true
home of necessity and incompatibility is the
actual world about us. We pass to alleged a
priori statements applying to it.

"Whatever is coloured must be extended."[4] Now if we take the statement *by
itself* as containing an *intrinsic* necessity leading from subject to predicate, then there
must be something in color as just color
with its unique quality that produces a quite
different sort of entity, extension. Does anyone really believe so in cold blood? What
could show less family resemblance than
this zestful moving *quale* and dead inert
extension? Idealists who defend the implication generally say that it does not reside
in the proposition merely by itself but only
as member of the whole system of things.
And we can agree to this: color as applied to
actual bodies, gaseous, liquid, or solid, al-

4. Brand Blanshard, *The Nature of Thought* (London, Allen
& Unwin, 1939), II, 407.

ways goes with extension (though not conversely). As we said above, given the order
of nature, such implications hold. We shall
later ask whether we may deny the necessity
of that order. But even now it is not hard to
find evidence against necessity—particularly
in the present case of color and extension.
For there seems to be nothing impossible in
the *notion* of an unextended color, even
though it is not met in the *physical* world.
Most people, in fact, have *seen* unextended
color: flecks of brightness at least, sparks,
what we call "seeing stars" from a crack on
the head, or other minute spots and dots
having some slight tinge of color and no
apparent extent, only location. These little
dots, considered as *physical* stimuli in the
eyeball do indeed have area and volume; but
the point is that there is experience of color
which is not experience of extension. And if
so, there can be no a priori implication from
the one to the other. A world of colored
points is not an *impossible* world, whether
actual or not.

Or take the following, perhaps a case of a
priori necessity in physics. Energy cannot
be at once potential and kinetic. As the ball

hits the ground its downward motion ceases and passes through a zero phase and then rebounds upward; these three phases occupy different periods. In so far as the ball is in the potential state of contact, just so far it is not moving; so far as it is falling or rebounding it is not and cannot be quiescent. Potential is the opposite of kinetic; they cannot be combined. But what now does potential mean? It means two distinct things: (1) positively tending toward a definite future—the rebound of the ball—and (2) *not* actually presenting anything of that future, not *moving* down or up but just in contact with the ground and the elasticity working furiously within while not yet expressing itself in the ball's rebound. Plainly the second characteristic is not consistent with the kinetic: that is already laid down. Resting means nonmoving just as blue means not-red. We cannot call the one the other. Incompatibility here is just tautology. But the first trait, the productive tendency of potential energy, is indeed compatible with kinetic energy. We have a case of it in the law of inertia. A body in motion in a straight line continues so unless acted upon by some external force. Its present motion is the potency of its future motion: motion is at once itself and potential of its own repetition. It is in fact a self-repeater.

That a thing cannot be at rest and in motion at the same time is, as usually understood, a tautology. The statement means that in the same system or with reference to the same body or bodies motion and rest cannot coincide. For of course if A is and remains five feet away from B, then as between A and B there is no motion. *Remains* denies *moves*. Yet if we bring in another dimension, A may be moving in a circle around B as the center. Here again, a higher dimension is but a way of seeing that supposed incompatibles are not genuine incompatibles.

We say: a body cannot be in two places at once. Obviously this is pure tautology. *Body* means what occupies a definite position in space and no other at the same time. It is like saying that one place cannot be another place. This is the notorious tautology of the law of contradiction. But if we try to go further and say "*nothing* can be in two places at once," we are wrong. A universal such as a particular shade of red, may well be in two places at once. Or if you accept Aristotle's and Aquinas' dictum that in knowing the mind is, in a sense, its object, then mind is in two places at once. In order to prove that nothing can be in two places at once it would seem requisite first to prove that there is nothing real but body; and even then the statement is tautologous.

Again, nothing, it is said, can possess two colors at the same time and place, or two tones (two smells and tastes would probably be allowed). If a peony is red it cannot be blue; if an olive is green it cannot be red; if a note is high-pitched it cannot be low. And so on. But is not purple two colors at once? True, the quality of a pure red is not individually the quality of a pure blue; but the question is whether the two may coexist in a single complex sense-datum. And there seems to be no reason for denying it. But we need not insist on the point. There are other cases at hand. What of the green olive that is said to preclude redness? It is a curious fact that many people actually sense a red in olive green. Here is no mixture; the green is undamaged by the red, and yet both are sensed at the same time and place. But further, consider the phenomemon of luster. There the two colors seem to interpenetrate without loss of the specific quality of each: the gray sheen on the black surface or the white on the blue, etc. The patch *looks* to be a pure blue and a pure white, etc., at the same time. Surely there could be no clearer case. Or consider perception of sound. One would naturally say that a given tone cannot have a low and a high pitch at once. Our experience is quite otherwise. We need mention only the hearing of overtones in a single note—so difficult for the untrained ear, so clear to the practiced musician. Indeed, sense is more liberal than is commonly recognized. The rationalist tradition has degraded it as source of knowledge, but it is in many ways more suggestive than understanding as to the range of possibility in nature.

The above examples, however, lie more or less in the realm of the trivial. After all, what matters whether two colors may or may not coexist? We feel no strong prohibitions here. But come now to a field in which the path is straight and narrow, alternatives are excluded, strict observance of rules is enjoined; viz., morality. Surely morality is the very home of incompatibility: built on the notion of every deed but one being ruled out, no compromise accepted, no combinability of wrong and right action. If I love God, I cannot hate my fellow man; if I inflict needless pain, I cannot be just; look *not* upon the wine when it is red. Sincerity here *means* this and no other. Omnicompatibility is the proper definition of sin.

A man begs money from me. Should I give it? I *postulate* the moral law: help one another—this is a case of helping another—therefore. Doubtless we think most moral issues out this way: the way of the syllogism which starts from the major premise of an assumed principle. The ruling out of the alternative is but a tautology. If helping is right, denial of help is wrong. If an orange is yellow, we must not deny that it is yellow. That is not incompatibility between two *different* things.

True, the case is often not so simple. There are many conscientious men to whom the law "help one another" would not imply giving to the beggar; probably a truer help would lie in questioning, learning his situation, character, etc., and getting him a responsible job. Perhaps, having lost a series of jobs through unlucky chance, he has also lost the self-confidence that goes with employment. Very well, the conscientious man decides not to give the beggar money but to give him a position of which he knows. And we say the man is thinking out the implicates of the moral law. Now in all this reasoning there are just two methods used. One is that of the syllogism, as already seen above. The other consists in appealing to the laws of the order in which we live: in this case to a particular psychological law, that consciousness of work done gives a helpful self-confidence. This is just a fact— the way most men are constituted. The logical procedure throughout is precisely what we have repeatedly found above: the implications and incompatibles we find are those that don't fit the constituted order of nature or the already assumed moral law. Intrinsic necessity and incompatibility are no more at home in morality than in psychology or physics.

Consider the famous Kantian example where the author deduces from the principle

of universality the more specific rule that
lying is wrong. Thus:

When I think myself in want of money, I will
borrow money and promise to repay it, although
I know that I never can do so. . . . How would it
be if my maxim were a universal law? Then I see
at once that it could never hold . . . but would
necessarily contradict itself . . . since no one
would consider that anything was promised to
him but would ridicule such statements as vain
pretences.[5]

The reasoning has been criticized by many:
the essence of the criticism[6] is that the result
is *not* deduced from the principle of universality alone, but also from the actual
psychological make-up of man. The point is
old enough to need no laboring. Here again
we find no specific implication.

What then of the implication of freedom?
You ought, therefore, you can. Responsi-
bility entails free choice. True, some deny
this; and that suggests a doubt of the implication. But let us grant it for the argument's
sake. Have we not then a synthetic judgment here? Is not free choice a different thing

5. T. K. Abbott, *Kant's Theory of Ethics* (4th ed. London,
Longmans, Green, 1889), p. 40.
6. Wallace, *The Logic of Hegel* (2d ed.), II, 111.

from a moral value? Love is a moral value, but love and free choice are not the same thing. Parents love their children, and parental love is a high moral value, but parents do not have any free choice in the matter, parental love being instinctive. Yet surely the answer is obvious. Grant that parental love is a moral value and that it does not involve free choice; then certainly the *general* implication alleged in Kant's dictum does not hold. It holds only in cases where men have the power to choose. The dictum simply emphasizes the fact that if one is confronted by a duty, then no matter how difficult its performance may be, he always has the power to do it. We don't call it a duty when it is easy and natural, no matter how good it may be. Duty is a word denoting conduct which is good, difficult, and yet within our power. In short the alleged entailment is a pure tautology.

But as yet we have been talking about reality piecemeal: the sense-qualities of things—the moral law in man's heart. We now, and finally, ask whether taken as a whole and in general the very notion of reality does not have certain implications.

Many have thought it does: these are the metaphysicians with their diverse claims. For instance, some assert that reality must be ultimately one, stable, permanent, and mind; and though on the face of things we find plurality, flux, and bodies, these cannot be ultimately real, being ruled out by the former. Others, again, affirming the reality of flux, plurality, etc., feel bound to deny the correlative traits. As we saw at the outset, here the compatibility-view bears directly on the life of metaphysics. If there is genuine inconsistency between these opposing factions—and the evidence of history shows each faction persisting with undiminished vigor—then surely the sceptic is right; the philosophic enterprise is hopeless. But our thesis, of course, is that these traits are not ruled out by their opposites, both being ultimately real.

Let us call the correlatives in each pair polars or polar opposites. Of these we have three outstanding pairs: one and many, flux and permanence, body and mind. Each pair embodies one of the great perennial issues: monism versus pluralism or dualism, process versus fixed eternal being, idealism versus materialism. Of these we should begin with the one–many couple. For obviously the compatibility of the other polars turns on the compatibility of one with two or more. Reality cannot ultimately be both process and permanent, or both body and mind, unless it can be both one and two; one perhaps in the sense of the genus *real*, and two or more in the sense of the species, this or that *kind* of real. Still less could the polar opposites combine in a single being, as in man who seems to be both body and mind in one. And another reason for the priority of the one–many issue is that the idealists themselves split on it. Monist (Hegelian) idealism denies the ultimate plurality of mind; personal idealism affirms it and denies the one all-inclusive absolute mind; a momentous conflict indeed, in its bearing on ethical standards and theism.

We take first, then, the one–many problem.

At the very start we find a certain obscuring of the issue by the monists. They claim to include all that the pluralist really wants— the reality of the finite persons—in the one absolute spirit. But the point is that they do so only by virtue of the organic principle;

and the organic principle denies the *ultimate* validity of the finite, which is the very thing the pluralist affirms. The important thing here is to distinguish between the ultimate and the derived or proximate reality. The absolutist may well admit (with Hegel, Bradley, etc.) that God needs the finite manifestations in order to be God, that the one needs the many in order to be one, and so on. But when he says *needs* he is but repeating his claim of organic unity. The pluralist denies this need—not, of course, wholly and throughout the universe, but as an unavoidable postulate or proved thesis holding in every aspect and department of being. The issue remains. To put it in another way: the absolutist may well admit the *relative* independence of finite selves, as witnessed in their free choices; he may even admit the apparent chance in the physical world, as testified to by certain doctrines of present-day physics. But he rescues himself by calling these phenomena lower degrees of reality, valid for relatively narrow or abstract points of view. His doctrine of degrees of reality helps him to include, indeed, many other metaphysical theses than his own, by assigning them to this or that limited perspective of the world. But always he insists that *ultimate* reality is and must be one system. And this is precisely what the pluralist denies. At least he denies the *must be*. The issue remains; for it is an issue between ultimates. Are these ultimates, one and many, incompatible?

The monist declares that independence between many is prevented from being ultimate because organic unity or system is a necessity of being. It is implied in the very meaning of intelligibility or intelligible reality. To understand anything is to see it as member of a whole or system. If he is right, we should expect to find an implication leading from any isolated part to other parts and finally to the system as one total. So we must ask, what is the evidence for such an implication? We have examined case after case of alleged implication between particular facts (color implies extension, ought implies freedom, etc.) and between isolated propositions (in mathematics) and found nothing but tautology. By all the evidence we can summon, there are no genuine logical implications.

But this isn't the whole story. For as a matter of fact the monist himself admits the point; if we seek within the unique essence of some abstract quality such as the color blue to find some logical finger pointing to the unique essence of red, or wet, or round, or anything else, we seek in vain. So Bosanquet: "An assertion of implications following upon a supposition which is in no way attached to an underlying real system, I do not believe to have a meaning."[7] It is the underlying whole system which alone guarantees the necessary connections.

The question then is: what is the evidence for this whole system? Empirical evidence furnished by the sciences is admittedly insufficient, though helpful; for, as the idealist himself insists, it can never justify an inference to the universal proposition that *all* things and events form a system of necessarily connected aspects. Sooner or later he must resort to an axiom or postulate, a priori certain: system alone is intelligibility, alone rational, alone credible for the thinker. It is the very nature of logical thought. Now notice this: he is trying to show that system

7. Blanshard, *op. cit.*, II, 431–432.

is inherent in logical thought. To show it, he ought to give evidence, drawn from the process of thought, that thought actually *uses* the notion of system, actually deals with implications. But we have seen above that thought does not do so: the more thoughtful and the less empirical it is—as in mathematics in contrast with physics—the *less* obviously implicative and the *more* nearly tautologous it becomes. If then all reasoning, so far as we can see, is nonimplicative, how can we say that system is a presupposition of rational thought? If there is no specific instance of a purely logical necessary connection, how declare that a whole of necessarily connected parts is an inescapable postulate of logical inquiry? No, when the crux of universality comes, the idealist does not offer the one kind of evidence he needs: he does not produce one single instance of logical necessity. Failing such instances, logical necessity becomes meaningless.

True, he will answer that experience presents to us many wholes, all more or less systematic: and for an impressive example, the inorganic world with its laws of motion, radiation, etc. We have already agreed that there is a high degree of order in nature, and necessity, too, in the causal connections. But, as the monists admit, the necessity that makes the second billiard ball move after the first hits it, is not due just to the motion of the first, but to the *total* systematic order. So the question returns: is there such an order, from which the particular causes draw their strength? Given it certainly is not—no monist would say that. Implied it cannot be, for there is no such thing as implication—*unless* this is the one case of it: but if it were, how should we recognize it, having never yet met implication?

Here the monist will play his last card— last because most abstract. How, he will say, could you assert that there is *no* logical implication unless you already knew what it meant? So it must be a positive, meaningful notion. But note: what we have done is to take cases of *alleged* logical implication—we not knowing what it might mean—and to show that they are cases of tautology or of the actual *given* order. We presupposed nothing; we found no meaning peculiar to logical implication. No, the causal necessities of nature are a mighty world-order so far as they go—but their might is not anything that logical analysis can lay bare in the causes. No deduction can tell why bodies fall, no induction can guarantee that they must fall. The power of nature is not definable in theoretical terms: it is directly experienced in our active efforts and not otherwise. Lift a heavy weight and you sense the causality of gravitation. You know that power and force are there. Vision or hearing, the contemplative senses, would never give that knowledge. But the rationalist philosopher, falling into the narrow perspective of the merely contemplative, neglects the knowledge gained from active intercourse with reality, and interprets power as a thought-entity, logical necessity, producing effects by its unique mode implication, spinning one meaning out of the bowels of another. This, we may take it, is the origin of that strange monster which breeds philosophical intolerance and enmity, the notion of ultimate incompatibles. The rationalist is worshiping a thought-idol. And as he offers no evidence we can but pronounce him a dogmatist. He is fulminating a dictum from the high command of the contemplative life.

If then there is no necessity of total system, there is nothing to deny ultimately independent terms. Nay more, there is nothing to deny that one and the same term is in some ways determined by causes, in other ways free. A coin, spun by the hand, may *add* to the velocity and direction thereby imparted, certain independent variations of its own.

But if ultimate plurality is not ruled out, is it compatible with ultimate unity? Here enter the dialecticians with their contradictions of one–many, same–different, etc. On the authority of this group, we may take it that the one–many is the typical form.

Bosanquet said it: "Contradiction consists in 'differents' being ascribed to the same term, while no distinction is alleged within that term such as to make it capable of receiving them."[8] And Bradley too: "The simple identification of the diverse is precisely that which one means by contradiction."[9] Simple and ultimate oneness comports not with simple and ultimate manyness. To avoid self-contradiction we must see the one

8. B. Bosanquet, *Logic* (2d ed.), I, 224.
9. *Mind* (1909), p. 496.

as not simple, but implicitly many, and conversely.

Note now that these statements tacitly assume the postulate of system. They say: what is one cannot be two or more unless there is something about oneness that *implies* manyness, and conversely; unless, that is, the predicate can be *deduced* from the subject. It is the same old ghost, and as before set up in a dogmatic affirmation. Of course, we answer, not only is there no need whatever for deducing twoness or manyness out of what is one, but such deduction is meaningless. Or we may put the monist's view in another way: the meaning of oneness is eternally *different* from the meaning of manyness—how then can they belong to the *same* subject? And it is well to put it thus, for it shows us that he lives and moves in the realm of meanings. For him, existence is a meaning. We have here but another side of the same idol: existence is wholly, exclusively, a thought-object—the philosophomorphic taint again. And again we answer, existence is not merely object of theory and contemplation but also of action and insight, and thus is more than meaning. Two meanings, any number of meanings, may be as *disparate* as you please, yet exist in one substance. In fact, substance means compatibility.

The bottom then on which the dialectical contradictions rest is the postulate of rational system. If this bottom is knocked from under they have no standing. One and the same thing or event or process or term or what not may be ultimately one and ultimately many. There is no principle to forbid the banns; and what is not forbidden is permitted. Yes, monist, dualist, and pluralist may all have ultimate truth. How far each does have it is matter for specific evidence.

Let us repeat: the bottom postulate has been knocked away. Not only have we found no instances of rational necessity; the notion itself is meaningless. It can't be *elucidated* by thought. It was indeed legitimately born in the fluid region of man's active intercourse with nature; for man must respect the powers of nature's order. But when transferred by the thinker to his lofty peak above the atmosphere, it dies like a fish out of water. There is no air for it to breathe. There is no content in the notion of ultimate necessity on which thought can expatiate.

Order is not self-existent; it is made, a fiat, a creature. Any one order, being made, may be unmade, superseded by another or mingled with another.

If present-day philosophers with empirical interests feel that this discussion of dialectical subtleties is needless, let them be reminded that they, too, need liberation from the dogma of incompatibles. The modern naturalist would not admit to an ultimate irreducible mind a validity equal to that of the behaving human organism; the revolter against monist idealism would not agree that there can be a rigidly determined world order. Practically all parties find their own ultimates incompatible with the ultimateness of the other ultimates.

In general, then, we may say that any two terms may be ultimate predicates of one and the same thing. At any rate, their twoness and its oneness do not conflict. But does this hold of the *specific* polars with which we are here concerned? Are process and stable permanence compatible? Are body and mind taken as irreducibly disparate, combinable in one individual?

Take then the former problem; the polars flux and permanence. We are told that any real being must be itself and no other; for the idealist this being is an individual mind, for the materialist the ultimate atoms, perhaps, or the units of radiant energy, for the scholastic the substantial forms, whether separate or embodied in prime matter. All agree, combating the modern process-metaphysic, that whatever loses its self-identity has not ultimate reality. This Greek insight is common to all three types: reality is a term or terms, self-identical, stable through change or even apart from it. Change is loss of being, weakness, inability to maintain one's identity. And the two are obviously incompatible. Ultimate being excludes ultimate process, and conversely. And on the other hand, the process-view denies the rigidly permanent, whether an unchanging God or a substantial form corporeal, human or other, or a physical atom, or an immortal soul. So far from being a self-identical term, the real is neither self-identical nor a term. It is a relation, the relation of passage; the only static terms are the unreal concepts which thought abstracts from the flowing events.

Surely this is a sharper opposition than

the one–many. Consider now the attitude of
the three older types. We see at once that
they confuse the ancient notion of process,
usually attributed to Heraclitus, with the
modern, defended by Bergson and others.
We made this distinction in Chapter III. To
the former, change is indeed loss of self-
identity, subtraction; when a man's body
dies, or water is dissolved into H and O,
these show a lack of power to be, a taint of
unreality. And the Greek masters, viewing
change thus, could not but take permanence
alone as the hallmark of reality; the two
notions were defined at the beginning as
contradicting. But the modern notion treats
of change as gain of being, as addition.
Duration is endurance plus novelty. This
incremental change is not destruction but
construction. Life and mind particularly
manifest it. I remember my past, to a degree
I re-live it, adding and fusing it in my present
feeling. So, too, in the evolution of species.
The later preserve many of the functions of
the earlier and lower, adding to them their
own novel ways. Here is no loss of the title
to ultimate reality, but rather the cue to
more and more reality. The contradiction

between permanence and change is removed.

No, there is no necessary incompatibility between flux and permanence. Both may be ultimately real. The axiom of the three older types is that of static self-identity; every real being must be itself and no other. The axiom of the modern type is: everything is what it is to be. The older views at once proceed to take their axiom in exclusion; nothing can change without *ceasing* to be what it was. The modern view has found a way of avoiding this exclusion: things may take on new traits without losing the old. Both axioms may be accepted. The standard illustration is Bergson's spiral-formed snowball.

And so the process-view is just as wrong in denying the Greek insight as are the older types in denying the new insight. Endless flux may heap up permanent gains, resources ever present undiminished, real because practically available, in man's mind and the powers of nature. Nay more, there is no ground for denying the unchanging static. Every order is subject to change: equally the changing order of nature may in part change its own habit of change. It may, for instance —for aught we know—generate in the inor-

ganic a group of entities that remain on,
unaffected internally by external changes.
Such permanent atoms cannot be ruled out
a priori. Surely the process-type, with its
hatred of a priori fixture, would be the last
to deny the possibility of a static reality.

In fact, is it not at once evident that no
two things, essences, meanings, so far as they
are *two* or *different*, can be incompatible? For
if they are each just itself and no other, how
can either go out of itself and affect in any way
the other? It is the old argument of Leibniz,
of pluralism and theism. As one monad cannot enter into another, so it cannot just of
itself influence another, either to preserve it
or change it or destroy it. Again it is the
simple logic of self-identity, the basis of all
term-philosophy. If anything enters into the
very essence or being of something else, it
so far loses its identity. Hence no real being
(which must remain self-identical) can get
outside itself and set up a disturbance within
another real being, inhibiting, conflicting
with, that latter. In fact, this is the bedrock
of our thesis, the simple elementary basis of
its whole train of thought. It seems so simple and so elementary as to warrant the

universal statement that no two entities can be incompatible: perhaps the only genuinely a priori statement that can be made. But after all, this is dialectics: let us now come to the specific, concrete problem of the third couple, the mind–body problem.

The problem is twofold: (1) How can one and the same individual or person be both mind and body? (2) How can there be interaction between the two?

The first question is easily answered. If any two meanings may coexist, if so far as they are just ultimately different neither one can of itself exercise any influence, constructive or destructive, on the other, then certainly there is nothing impossible in a human individual being both. Find the mind–body disparateness as extreme as you please; it makes no difference. Show that mind has properties which the very nature of body rules out; e.g., minds remember and infer and feel good and bad, while bodies are incapable of referring to the past in memory or the future in hope or dread. Even so, there is no contradiction in a human body and brain being welded with a conscious mind that can do things which the stuff of body and brain could never do. My hand can never learn to see, but who would find a contradiction in adding the power of the eye to that of the hand in the single living body? The monist and dualist may both be right.

The problem of interaction looks harder. And why? Because the question of monism versus dualism turns wholly on the dialectical one–many problem, while the question of interaction has to do with the specific facts of our actual world order. How can a mind which is not physical move its physical body when the laws of conservation of energy and momentum forbid the addition of new energy and even the shifting of the direction of a nerve-current? But there are really two questions concealed in this. One of them is: how could it be logically possible for two entities so utterly different as mind and body to act on each other? The other is: if the conservation of energy, etc., is a *proved fact*, how can mind initiate a bodily movement? The former question is concerned with a priori possibility, the latter with the existing order of nature. Now when we ask whether the law of conservation is verified fact in the realm of the human mind–body we can answer only by experiment and observation. Hitherto, experiment and observation have been altogether too unrefined to permit a decision.

Even the very careful experiments of Atwater and Benedict fall so far short of the precision reached in the electrodynamic field that we can hardly draw a conclusion. But probably the antidualist philosophers are not banking very much on this question of fact. What makes them reject the common-sense dualist interaction is rather the logical impossibility (as they view it) of causal relation between the bodiless and the body. They recall Clifford's analogy of the sentiment of amity between guard and stoker holding the engine and cars together. They feel that the cause must, as Spinoza had said,[10] have something in common with its effect, some likeness of nature. For a thought to beget a movement would be worse than for a man to beget a sheep. As Hocking said, interaction would be anomalous causation.

Now be it submitted that this is just one of those old incompatibles that we pored

10. *Ethics* (London, J. M. Dent & Sons, 1930), Axiom 5, pt. I.

over so long. Why should the cause have a likeness of nature to the effect? It is not merely that is usually *does*: we are told that it *ought* to. Is it not plain that the feeling is due to a logical demand? The effect is what is effected, that is ex-factum, made out of the cause, as the child is made out of the body of the parent. Causality would not be rational unless the thing made were of the same stuff as its maker. The effect must be deducible from the cause, and from one thing you cannot deduce something of a quite different nature. The feeling here is at bottom the same one that sways the monist: demand for logical implication. But if there is no logical implication from one fact to a different fact, there is no reason why the cause *must* be like the effect. Nature as we have seen is an order of power, of given laws whose efficiency comes not from the things and events but from some external source. And of power we know no a priori limitation.

It is all a question of fact. Are the causes we come across in our intercourse with nature, including ourselves, like their effects, or aren't they? Now notice that the primary experience we have of causality is our own felt desire and effort to move our own limbs and with them external bodies. Interaction is thus given as it were at the outset of our lives and it continues so given until we die. Interaction is the *fons et origo* of causal relation. Later we learn that in the physical world cause and effect very closely resemble each other. Motion gives rise to motion, potential energy to kinetic, and so on. And the physical sciences have discovered so vast an array of this kind—the whole range of stellar universe so far as we know it—that we are just overawed. The primary experience of causation seems of so puny import, so exceptional, that we either quite forget it or call it a remnant of primitive animism. Had we reflected further, we should have seen that in nature's laws there is no logical necessity whatsoever and that the likeness between cause and effect, instead of revealing a realm of gigantic causal power, displays one of minimum causal power. So to speak, the inorganic physical causes are not productive enough—powerful enough, as power means productivity and fertility—to generate much more than a repetition of themselves. The motion of a billiard ball gives rise only to the similar motion of another; the radiant energy of light, striking a surface, merely produces a change in its own direction. A richer, more powerful causality, perhaps that of living things, generates qualities not found in the simple self-repeaters of the inorganic. And a still more powerful causality is that of mind, which rearranges material things and processes to bring forth the qualities of utility, beauty, and other forms which in turn minister to man's mind. So interaction is really a higher and fuller kind of causality—that is of productive power—than is to be found in the inorganic world. It is a mystery and an anomaly only to those who rest at the lower level of causality, where the passage from cause to effect is almost a tautology; so nearly a tautology indeed, that the rationalist is fooled into thinking the effect can be deduced from the cause. For, although he does not realize it, all deduction is tautology.

See then how natural it is for the contemplative thinker to get bogged by the problem of interaction. His profession disinclines him more and more to consult the experiences of his active life; he is the visualizing metaphysician, idolizing the categories of thought into the entity rational implication. Now inorganic nature *is* a region of necessity— we have to respect its power in daily life. The thinker inevitably views this necessity from his own perspective; it becomes for him a matter of rational implication. And the laws of the inorganic are *almost* tautologous; the effects (motions, attractions, etc.) differ so little from the causes (other motions, etc.) that the rationalist has hope of some-time actually deducing the effect from the cause. That is why he emphasizes the com-monness of nature between effect and cause. That is why Spinoza, deeply impressed by the mechanistic order of physical nature, and a rationalist of rationalists in his quiet con-templation of life, postulated that cause and effect must have something in common. But it would be better to put the thing nega-tively: the *less* causality (productiveness) there is, the more the effect will be like the cause. Yet the contemplative thinker, for whom the category of productive power is obsolescent, can hardly help taking this least of all causal relations as the type; and so for him the mind–body dualism and interaction become insoluble paradoxes.

Interaction is not a mystery, because it contravenes no necessary principles. The conception of causation that *seems* to go against it is a false and low-level one, conjured up by the thinker's idol of rational implication. The ghost reappears once more, this time dressed in the garments of natural science. And in that garb most thinkers of today begin to fear him. Even thinkers outside the idealist group turn against dualistic interaction; for they respect and fear what they think is the proved scientific meaning of causal connection. So the materialists, who will not admit that mind can add new energy to any physical system; so the process-group, who are driven to their experience-monism because they think the Cartesian dualism and interaction is not scientifically intelligible. But science uses no preconceived notion of causal connection except regular repetition or uniform sequence. It simply records instance after instance of the order it finds in nature. Only when the scientist turns philosopher does he fill out the notion of cause-effect into necessary implication or identity of pattern or what not. No, it is not respect for the results of physics that need make one deny the Cartesian dualism.

So much for the compatibility of mind and body and interaction between them, in constituting a single individual.

Notice, however, that so far no specific account is offered of the nature of their union. They may turn out to be related as form and matter, as the modern Thomists say. They may be two irreducible and ultimate kinds of substance, functioning together in man in a not quite harmonious unity—a view nearer to the Cartesian dualism. They may be two aspects of one thing, analogous to inner and outer or potential and kinetic—as the panpsychist might claim. Or they may differ solely as ways of behaving in one and the same body or chain of experience, as the process-view would hold. The point is that none of these offers in principle any incompatibility which could rule it out at the beginning.

But let us have no illusions. The professional philosopher will fight to the last ditch before giving up his loved idol—loved because he constructed it himself—the idol of rational implication. He will ever insist that causality *must* carry such implication, and even though we cannot demonstrate it in any specific case, reason must postulate it, take it as article of faith or dogma. And so he will find the notion of power here used, to be meaningless or self-contradictory. He will brand our thesis of compatibility as irrationalism. He will say that we try to defeat the whole philosophic enterprise. And in particular, that we have not made inter-action intelligible; we have pointed out no trait in mind which would suggest, still less imply, a bodily movement. He might admit that we were right about the consistency of the one–many or even of the changing per-manent, for after all these are dialectical matters; but as a rational being he will hardly admit that common-sense interaction is the final word. And what we are here saying is no mere inference; it is the evidence of history. The perennial types of meta-physic—idealism, scholasticism, material-ism, process—all deny interaction. The com-mon-sense dualism, which accepts it, has never formed a characteristic type of system in the Occident. There is something repugnant to the philosopher (except for the practical Chinese) in the notion of a power not definable in terms of logical implication. Such power, we may expect all the types to declare, is meaningless.

But how interesting! *Meaningless*. Just what the implicationist would be expected to say. For the meaning of anything consists for him in drawing out the implications. Rain means wet ground, the law of inertia means continued motion. Where he can find no implications, he finds no meaning. Practical power contains no implication from cause to effect. Hence it is meaningless, irrational, nonsense. He is really condemning the notion, not because he finds it inconsistent with acknowledged facts, but because it is not in accord with his idol. He is only reiterating his dogma. "Give a dog a bad name and hang him," says the proverb.

No, there is no just accusation here. Reality is what we in our active life meet and in our quiet observation see, and we can lay down beforehand no test of what that may be. Shall we then say that causal laws might

connect any two things whatsoever? Could
$\sqrt{-1}$ give birth to an elephant?

There is in any one event or thing or term
no meaning peculiar to itself which will spin
out some other. There is no power intrinsic
to the single entity or process. There is
power indeed, for we have daily witness of
the many powers lodged in the stones, the
trees, the air, the water, the bodies and
minds of animals and of our fellow men. But
the power cannot be traced to the internal
make-up of these causes, when we consider
them by themselves, in abstraction, as isolated terms. It is then a derived power. It
comes from some external source or sources.
It is given to the particular things, bestowed
on them from without. Leibniz was not so
far wrong as the monists think, in his Pre-
established Harmony. The causality exer-
cised by stones, trees, and men is given to
them; they have no a priori claim on it. Our
minds are able to move our bodies because
the power is given them. What powers are
given to man, or to anything else, can be
discovered only by action, by experiment.
Action and experiment tell us, so far as we
can see, that interaction is a fact. Only a

preconceived theory, an idol fabricated by a dogmatic reason, can prevent us from admitting it. Only such a theory can find interaction, and in general power, a mystery, unintelligible and irrational. For only that is irrational in the bad sense which goes *against* reason, and here reason has nothing which fact can go against.

The irony of the situation is that the monist does believe that $\sqrt{-1}$ gives birth to an elephant, except that he would not say *gives birth* but *necessarily involves*. For to him all parts of reality imply one another. But we who accept the given order of nature as much as he does, do not make it into an all-embracing necessary system, and we can accept with natural piety the order so far as it is verified by the sciences, and also the independence of some phenomena from others, if also verified. We can say that in our given order, mathematical imaginaries are quite irrelevant to the generation of elephants.

Nevertheless, however unwarranted the rationalist's claim of deducing the effect out of the cause, there is a sense in which he may be right. There may be a positive core of truth in his conviction that like causes like; truth which the pious empiricist can well admit. Suppose the rationalist grants that there is nothing in mind which of itself gives rise to a bodily movement, nothing in bodies which of itself makes them gravitate, and that the order of nature is imposed on it from without. Still his belief in causal likeness may be sound. It is possible that the *connection* between cause and effect is due to some being or beings of a nature like to both. Suppose for example, the theist is right, and there is a first cause of all that is. Suppose this first cause contains in himself, all the positive traits of all things, in one individual being. Suppose then that he creates a world quite other than himself—creating by sheer power as the empiricist says— and imposes on it laws connecting specific causes and effects. Then these laws imitate his nature; for the particular cause-effect connections were, like all other possibles, already in that nature, and the positive essences of every cause and every effect as well. The creatures imitate the creator. Like makes like.

To summarize the result of these chapters.

(1) All the elements of reality are compatible with one another. This, if we realized it, would abolish the wasteful civil war within the philosopher's fold, and free his energies for constructive discovery of nature's ways, and an increasingly fruitful plan for human life. (2) But further: there is, as the present-day process-view suggests, evidence that nature herself is putting forth ever new permutations and combinations of her elements, joining more and more things that formerly seemed uncombinable—in brief, there is a principle of growth in nature. It is the philosopher's task to emulate this growth. In so doing, he is well aware that new perspectives of which he now can little dream will be forthcoming. He will then be the first of his kind to affirm the poet's profound saying, "There are more things in heaven and earth . . . than are dreamt of in our philosophy." But those things will add to, and not refute, the truths already verified.